Business Handbook on Due Diligence in the Cocoa Sector

ADDRESSING CHILD LABOUR AND FORCED LABOUR

OECD
BETTER POLICIES FOR BETTER LIVES

Please cite this publication as:
OECD (2023), *Business Handbook on Due Diligence in the Cocoa Sector: Addressing Child Labour and Forced Labour*, OECD Publishing, Paris, https://doi.org/10.1787/79812d6f-en.

ISBN 978-92-64-35210-0 (print)
ISBN 978-92-64-93229-6 (pdf)
ISBN 978-92-64-91455-1 (HTML)
ISBN 978-92-64-81829-3 (epub)

Photo credits: Cover © International Cocoa Initiative.

Corrigenda to OECD publications may be found on line at: www.oecd.org/about/publishing/corrigenda.htm.

Foreword

The Business Handbook on Due Diligence in the Cocoa Sector: Addressing Child Labour and Forced Labour (Handbook) helps companies identify, prevent and address child labour and forced labour risks in the cocoa sector. The Handbook is based on the UN Guiding Principles for Business and Human Rights (UNGPs), the ILO Conventions on child labour and forced labour, the OECD Guidelines for Multinational Enterprises (OECD Guidelines for MNEs), and the OECD recommendations on risk-based due diligence detailed in the OECD Due Diligence Guidance for Responsible Business Conduct (OECD Due Diligence Guidance) and the OECD-FAO Guidance for Responsible Agricultural Supply Chains (OECD-FAO Guidance). Together these instruments are the leading international, government-backed standards on responsible business conduct and corporate due diligence.

The international community has committed to ending forced labour and eliminating child labour in all its forms by 2025. However, the world is still far from meeting this goal. The latest global estimates from the ILO indicate that 160 million children were in child labour in 2020 and 27.6 million adults and children were in forced labour in 2021. It is estimated that 70% of child labour takes place in the agricultural sector in subsistence and commercial farming and herding, typically as unpaid family labour.[1] Within the sector, cocoa producing countries in Africa and Latin America are flagged as producing cocoa with child labour (ILAB, 2022[1]). While forced labour is less prevalent than child labour in the cocoa supply chain, its impacts can be more serious.

In drafting this Handbook, the Organisation for Economic Co-operation and Development (OECD), the International Cocoa Initiative (ICI) and the Deutsche Gesellschaft für Internationale Zusammenarbeit GmbH (GIZ), convened a multi-stakeholder informal expert group (IEG) of 12 representatives from business, civil society, international organisations and other experts to provide substantive inputs to the Handbook and guide its development. The OECD and ICI also organised a workshop with stakeholders in Abidjan, Côte d'Ivoire in June 2022 and a virtual workshop in November 2022. In addition, an informal public consultation with stakeholders was launched in January 2023.

This Handbook was developed with financial support from the German Federal Ministry for Economic Co-operation and Development (BMZ) and the International Cocoa Initiative (ICI).

Table of contents

FIGURES

TABLES

Executive summary

The OECD-FAO Guidance for Responsible Agricultural Supply Chains (OECD-FAO Guidance) (OECD/FAO, 2016[2]) and the OECD Due Diligence Guidance for Responsible Business Conduct (OECD Due Diligence Guidance) (OECD, 2018[3]) help enterprises operationalise OECD risk-based due diligence consistent with internationally recognised standards on responsible business conduct such as the OECD Guidelines for Multinational Enterprises (OECD Guidelines for MNEs), the UN Guiding Principles on Business and Human Rights (UNGPs) and ILO conventions on labour. Implementing these recommendations can help enterprises avoid and address adverse impacts related to workers, human rights, the environment, bribery, consumers and corporate governance that may be associated with their operations and supply chains and other business relationships (OECD/FAO, 2021[4]).

While businesses are generally aware of the need to respect human rights and support responsible business conduct, the practical implementation of risk-based due diligence to identify, prevent and address risks and adverse impacts remains a challenge. Implementation challenges persist particularly in complex and fragmented supply chains such as in the agricultural sector. In addition, businesses often have limited experience in engaging civil society, worker representatives and government actors to support effective due diligence and risk mitigation strategies in line with expectations set out by the United Nations (UN), the OECD and the International Labour Organization (ILO).[2]

This Handbook addresses these gaps by focusing on child labour and forced labour, which are recognised as salient human rights issues in the cocoa sector. This Handbook illustrates how companies can operationalise OECD risk-based due diligence to address child labour and forced labour risks and impacts in the cocoa supply chain. It is anticipated that this Handbook can also inspire company due diligence to address additional human rights risks in other agricultural supply chains.

The Handbook does not provide new recommendations, but rather explains how OECD recommendations on risk-based due diligence can be applied to address child labour and forced labour by contextualising existing recommendations and directing users towards helpful sources related to addressing these risks.

Finally, although the Handbook addresses the challenge of due diligence in cocoa supply chains globally, most examples come from West Africa.

Why a Handbook?

Businesses operating in the cocoa sector are at risk of being linked to adverse impacts, in particular child labour and forced labour, through their operations, supply chains and business relationships.

While businesses are generally aware of the need to respect human rights and support responsible business conduct through risk-based due diligence, many still find it challenging to operationalise these expectations within their cocoa supply chains. The Handbook has been designed to help companies identify, prevent and address both risks and actual impacts relating to human rights in the cocoa sector, focusing on child labour and forced labour. Business can use this Handbook to translate responsible business commitments into action using OECD risk-based due diligence.

The Handbook:

- Promotes a common understanding of risks and impacts in cocoa supply chains, to help companies meet voluntary and mandatory standards on due diligence and commitments on child labour and forced labour.
- Provides clarity on how to operationalise existing OECD recommendations on due diligence in complex and fragmented supply chains in the cocoa sector.
- Provides sector-specific considerations, tips and examples for business to implement due diligence, including for small and medium-sized enterprises (SMEs).
- References existing resources available to companies that can be used to support due diligence and address child labour and forced labour in the sector.

Who is this Handbook for?

This Handbook is for companies in the cocoa sector operating at any stage of the supply chain, regardless of geographic location or company size. Given that human rights risks and impacts are present along the full cocoa supply chain, cocoa co-operatives and farmer organisations, cocoa traders and processors, chocolate manufacturers, confectionary brands and retailers who sell cocoa products may all find value in this Handbook.

How to use this Handbook?

This Handbook has been kept as concise as possible based on feedback from business users that have asked for targeted advice on how to operationalise the OECD risk-based due diligence framework.

To make the Handbook practical, each step of the OECD due diligence framework includes a set of strategic questions companies should ask when implementing each step. In addition, acknowledging that SMEs are the majority of businesses in the sector and may face specific challenges to operationalising risk-based due diligence, the Handbook provides tips specifically to SMEs.

Users are recommended to use this Handbook in conjunction with the key instruments on OECD risk-based due diligence published by the OECD: the OECD-FAO Guidance for Responsible Agricultural Supply Chains (OECD-FAO Guidance) (OECD/FAO, 2016[2]) and the OECD Due Diligence Guidance for Responsible Business Conduct (OECD Due Diligence Guidance) (OECD, 2018[3]). These two government-backed instruments provide corporate actors and investors the primary recommendations regarding international due diligence expectations and are the guiding texts on recommendations regarding OECD risk-based due diligence. Users of the Handbook are invited to go through the insights and tips provided in each chapter and review additional resources available on the website of the International Cocoa Initiative (ICI).[3]

Child labour and forced labour in the cocoa sector

This chapter introduces the definitions of child labour and forced labour, provides a general overview of the scale of the issue, and argues why businesses should care about human rights in the cocoa sector.

Understanding child labour and forced labour

Child labour and forced labour are both a symptom and a consequence of systemic poverty. These complex challenges are not limited to the cocoa sector and have several root causes, including poverty, lack of access to quality essential services and infrastructure such as education, health care, social protection; challenges with enforcing legal and regulatory frameworks; a lack of decent employment opportunities; gender inequality; low levels of adult labour (often linked to low wages in a given sector); challenges with access to land tenure; and the availability of effective corporate due diligence programmes.

Definition of child labour

Not all work carried out by children is child labour. According to the ILO, children's and adolescents' participation in economic work that does not affect their health and personal development or interfere with or prejudice their schooling or their participation in vocational orientation or training programmes is generally regarded as positive and therefore acceptable child work/light work. Child/light work is work that is generally non-hazardous, performed for fewer than 14 hours per week and by children aged 13 or older, when permitted by local law (ILO/IOE, 2015[5]).

Two ILO Conventions define child labour:

- The Minimum Age Convention 1973 (No. 138) defines "child labour" as work that deprives children of their childhood, their potential and their dignity, and that is harmful to their physical or mental development including by interfering with their education by depriving them of the opportunity to attend school; obliging them to leave school prematurely; or requiring them to attempt to combine school attendance with excessively long and heavy work. It also sets the minimum age for work at 15 years (13 years for light work), and 18 years for hazardous work (16 under certain strict conditions) (ILO, n.d.[6]).
- The Worst Forms of Child Labour Convention 1999 (No. 182) defines four categories of the worst forms of child labour (ILO, n.d.[7]):
  a) All forms of slavery or practices similar to slavery, such as the sale, trafficking of children, debt bondage and serfdom or compulsory labour, including forced or compulsory recruitment of children for use in armed conflict.
  b) The use, procuring or offering of a child for prostitution, for the production of pornography or for pornographic performances.
  c) The use, procuring or offering of a child for illicit activities, in particular for the production and trafficking of drugs as defined in the relevant international treaties.
  d) "Hazardous work" which, by its nature or the circumstances in which it is carried out, is likely to harm the health, safety or morals of children. The precise nature of those prohibited tasks is to be defined and reviewed by each country.

Categories a), b) and c) are known as *unconditional* forms of child labour, meaning they are prohibited without regard to the age of the child, the nature and the tasks executed, the conditions and circumstances in which those tasks are executed. Category d) is a conditional worst form of child labour, hence the need to be defined locally through a nationally defined list of hazardous activities.

In the cocoa sector, a majority of children involved in child labour are undertaking hazardous work, including carrying heavy loads, using dangerous tools and being exposed to pesticides. A small percentage of these children are reported to be in forced labour situations.

In addition, the UN's Convention on the Rights of the Child (UNCRC) adopted in 1989, protects children from economic exploitation including the right to be protected from work that is likely to be hazardous or to interfere with the child's education, or to be harmful to the child's health or physical, mental, spiritual, moral or social development; protects children from all forms of physical or mental violence, injury or abuse, neglect or negligent treatment, maltreatment or exploitation, including sexual abuse; and protects children from all forms of sexual exploitation and sexual abuse (UN, n.d.[8]).

Figure 1. Examples of hazardous child labour on cocoa farms

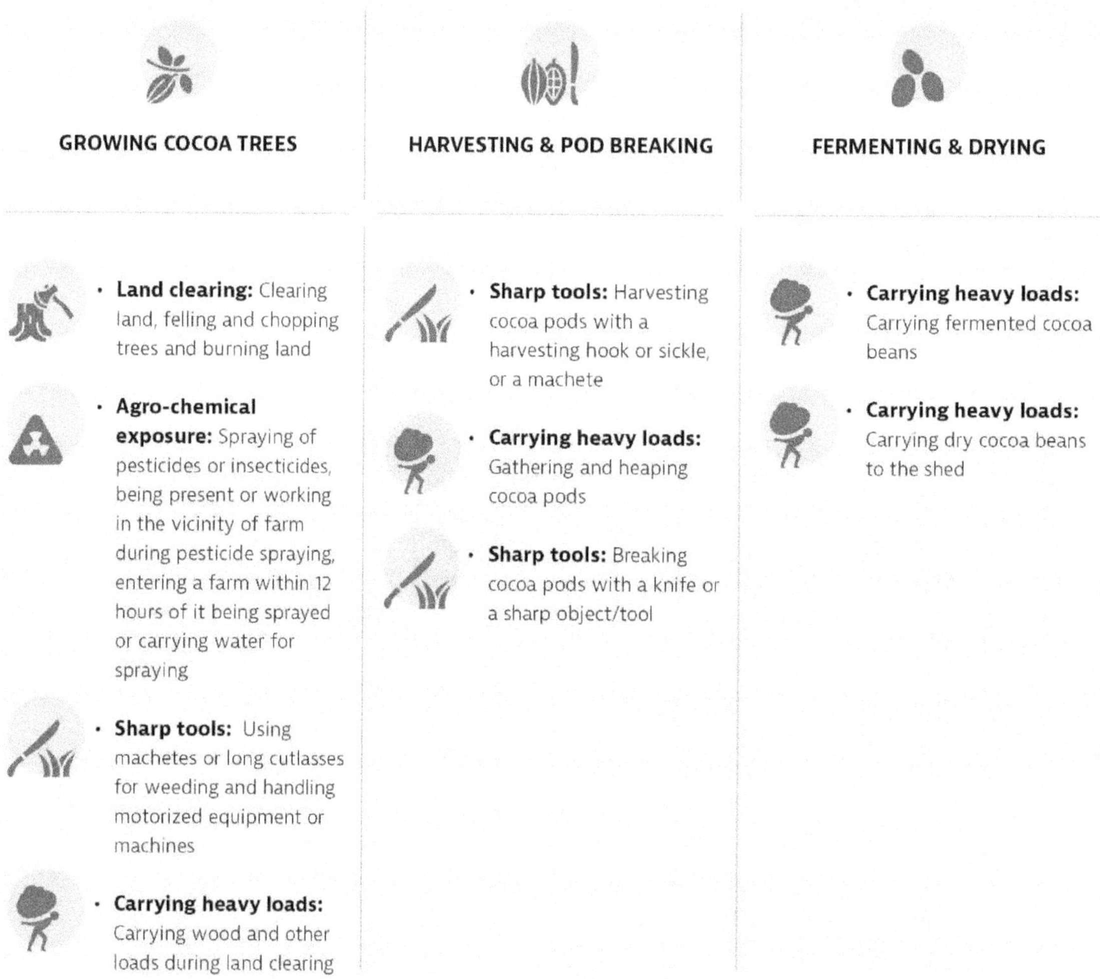

Source: Adapted from interviews conducted with farmers in Ghana and Cote d'Ivoire and Sadhu (2020[9]), *Assessing Progress in Reducing Child Labor in Cocoa Growing Areas of Côte d'Ivoire and Ghana*, https://www.norc.org/PDFs/Cocoa%20Report/NORC%202020%20Cocoa%20Report_English.pdf

Definition of forced labour

Forced labour is defined by ILO Convention No. 29 (1930) as "all work or service which is exacted from any person under the menace of any penalty and for which the said person has not offered himself voluntarily" (ILO, n.d.[10]). "Menace of any penalty" refers to the means of coercion used to impose work on someone against that person's will, during recruitment or once the person is working. "Involuntary work" refers to any work taking place without the free and informed consent of the worker. A forced labour situation is therefore determined by the nature of the relationship between the victim and the perpetrator and not by the type of activity performed. There must be both coercion and a lack of free and informed consent for work to be regarded as forced labour.

Forced labour can apply to both adults and children. Children are considered in forced labour when one or more of the following situations apply (ILO, 2018[11]):

- Work performed for one or both parents who are themselves in a situation of forced labour.
- Work performed under the menace of any penalty applied by a third party, either to the child directly or the child's parents.
- The child is performing work which can be classified under one of three types of the worst forms of child labour: a) all forms of slavery or practices similar to slavery, b) the use of a child for prostitution, production of pornography or for pornographic performances, c) the use of a child for illicit activities such as production and trafficking of drugs.

How prevalent is child labour and forced labour in the cocoa sector?

Cocoa is an important commodity in the agricultural sector, with cocoa beans being the major ingredient of chocolate. About 70% of the world's cocoa originates from Africa, with Côte d'Ivoire and Ghana being the leading producers accounting respectively for 44% and 16% of global cocoa production in 2019-20 (ICCO, 2022[12]). Southeast Asia and Oceania, and Latin America also contribute to global cocoa production at 6% and 19% respectively (ICCO, 2022[12]).

The international community has committed to "taking immediate and effective measures to eradicate forced labour, end modern slavery and human trafficking and secure the prohibition and elimination of the worst forms of child labour, including recruitment and use of child soldiers, and by 2025 end child labour in all its forms" (Alliance 8.7, 2018[13]). However, the latest global estimates indicate that 160 million children were still in child labour across all sectors in 2020, with 70% of all children in child labour (representing 112 million children) working in the agriculture sector (ILO/UNICEF, 2021[14]). The US Department of Labour provides data on the prevalence of child labour and forced labour in specific countries.[4]

Figure 2. Scale of child labour in the cocoa sector

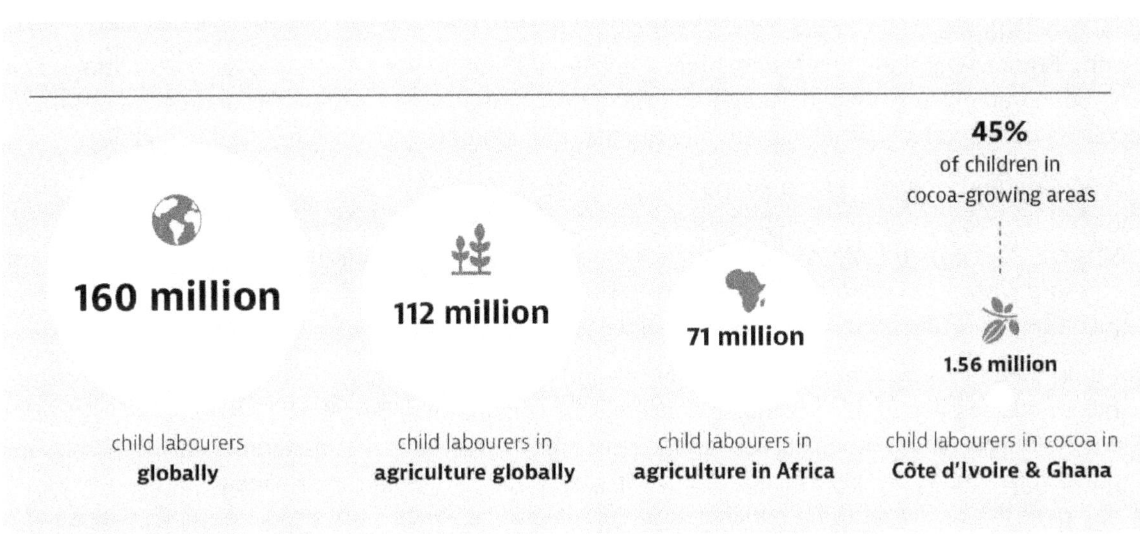

Source: ILO/UNICEF (2021[14]), Child Labour: Global estimates 2020, trends and the road forward, https://www.ilo.org/ipec/Informationresources/WCMS_797515/lang-en/index.htm; Sadhu (2020[9]), Assessing Progress in Reducing Child Labor in Cocoa Growing Areas of Côte d'Ivoire and Ghana, https://www.norc.org/PDFs/Cocoa%20Report/NORC%202020%20Cocoa%20Report_English.pdf

Figure 3. Scale of forced labour in the cocoa sector

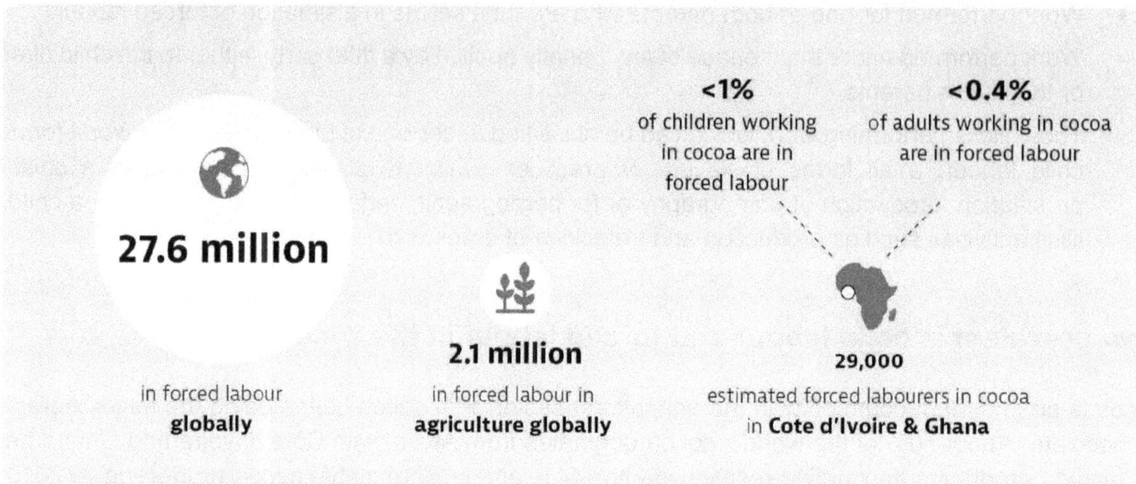

Source: ILO/Walk Free/IOM (2022[15]), Global Estimates Of Modern Slavery: Forced Labour And Forced Marriage, https://www.walkfree.org/reports/global-estimates-of-modern-slavery-2022/; Sadhu (2020[9]), Assessing Progress in Reducing Child Labor in Cocoa Growing Areas of Côte d'Ivoire and Ghana, https://www.norc.org/PDFs/Cocoa%20Report/NORC%202020%20Cocoa%20Report_English.pdf; Tulane University, Walk Free Foundation (2018[16]), The prevalence of forced labour and child labour in the cocoa sectors of Côte d'Ivoire and Ghana, https://www.cocoainitiative.org/knowledge-hub/resources/walk-free-foundation-study-prevalence-forced-labour-and-child-labour-cocoa.

What are the characteristics of the cocoa supply chain and how do they impact company due diligence efforts?

Globally 90% of cocoa is produced by smallholder farms ranging from five hectares or less (ICCO, n.d.[17]), representing 5 to six million farmers (Kozicka M., Tacconi F. , Horna D. , Gotor E., 2018[18]). Cocoa beans change hands multiple times in the supply chain, moving from producers to aggregators, to traders and exchanges, and then onto processors. Processors are typically located overseas, in countries such as Belgium, France, Germany, the Netherlands, Switzerland and the United States. Over 36% of the annual cocoa bean harvest is ground in Europe and nearly 8% in the United States. Ground cocoa is sent on to chocolate/cocoa product manufacturers and brands, and thereafter to retailers (ICCO, 2022[19]).

In Ghana, farmers mainly sell their cocoa beans to community-based procurement clerks that are contracted by licensed buying companies regulated by the Ghana Cocoa Board (COCOBOD) (Fairtrade Foundation, 2020[20]). In Côte d'Ivoire, farmers either sell their cocoa through a co-operative, or through local traders known as *pisteurs,* who typically trade with approximately 25 to 30 farmers. *Pisteurs* deliver the cocoa beans to larger licensed traders (Fairtrade Foundation, 2020[20]).

More than 50% of cocoa farmers in Côte d'Ivoire and Ghana are reported to be not part of co-operatives (up to 1.69 million people) and are thus a challenge for midstream and downstream companies to account for in their supply chain mapping and traceability efforts (Fairtrade Foundation, 2020[20]). While some companies have made progress in increasing transparency over their sourced cocoa, many are still lacking visibility over the origins and the conditions under which the beans were produced or harvested. Thus, implementing effective due diligence that identifies, prevents and addresses child labour and forced labour at scale remains a challenge for the sector.

Box 1. Why should businesses carry out due diligence?

When effectively applied, risk-based due diligence can help businesses identify and prevent adverse impacts on human rights, thus respecting international frameworks, demonstrating business efforts to investors and regulators, and contributing to the SDGs in a measurable way. Business carries out due diligence because of:

- **Commercial value:** Due diligence provides businesses with clarity on where risks are in the supply chain, enabling them to pro-actively get in front of problems, identify opportunities to meet customer and market needs and potentially build value. Integrating due diligence into corporate risk management systems helps strengthen the overall management of business and builds supplier and stakeholder engagement to increase business resilience. Increased transparency over the supply chain can also better position companies to access new capital and better financial terms.
- **Regulatory requirements:** Governments are increasingly legislating to oblige enterprises to conduct due diligence to identify and address human rights and environmental risks in global supply chains. In 2022, the European Commission published a draft Corporate Sustainability Due Diligence Directive (CSDDD), intended to become a leading standard for responsible business conduct, as well as a proposal to ban products made with forced labour from the EU market. Several European countries, such as France, Germany, Norway, Switzerland and the United Kingdom have introduced laws with different degrees of due diligence obligations for businesses. Outside Europe, similar legislative approaches have been adopted in Australia and the United States (UNICEF, 2022[21]).
- **Societal expectations:** Consumers, buyers, employees, and citizens expect companies to respect human rights as a minimum standard of "doing business". In the cocoa sector these expectations are especially high given the prevalence of child labour and the high rates of environmental degradation for a product which is considered as a "nice to have" or luxury item. Due diligence helps a company to "know and show" how it contributes positively to society, thereby helping protect its reputation.

OECD due diligence

This chapter introduces the OECD's due diligence framework and how companies can understand their responsibility vis-a-vis an adverse impact and what this implies in terms of company action.

What is due diligence?

The OECD has developed a risk-management framework for companies to identify, prevent, mitigate and account for how they address actual and potential adverse impacts, including on human rights, associated with their operations, supply chains and business relationships.

The framework, which is further elaborated in the OECD Due Diligence Guidance includes six measures of corporate due diligence to meet responsible business conduct (RBC) commitments:

1. To embed RBC into the company's policies and management systems
2. To identify actual or potential adverse impacts on RBC issues
3. Ceasing, preventing or mitigating RBC issues
4. Tracking implementation and results
5. Communicating how impacts are addressed
6. To enable remediation when appropriate

Due diligence should be sensitive to the needs of the most vulnerable groups and communities, including women.[5] In Côte d'Ivoire and Ghana, for example, studies suggest child labour is lower in communities where adult education levels, particularly women's, are higher (ICI, 2019[22]).

The OECD-FAO Guidance which should be used in conjunction with the OECD Due Diligence Guidance and this Handbook, includes detailed recommendations on how companies and investors operating in the agricultural sector can use due diligence to prevent and address social, environmental and governance risks and harms relevant to agricultural supply chains including child labour and forced labour.

Figure 4. OECD due diligence framework and supporting measures

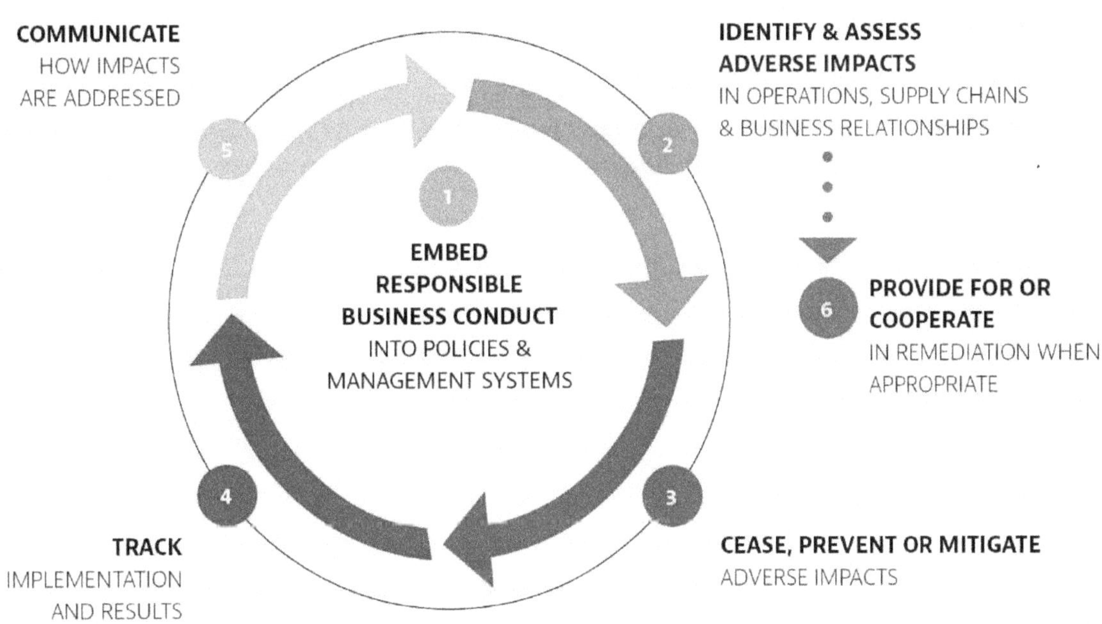

Source: OECD (2018[3]), OECD Due Diligence Guidance for Responsible Business Conduct, http://mneguidelines.oecd.org/OECD-Due-Diligence-Guidance-for-Responsible-Business-Conduct.pdf

Box 2. What is meant by "Adverse Impacts" and "Risk"?

The OECD Guidelines for MNEs acknowledge that business can make many positive contributions to economies and local communities. However, they also recognise that business activities may result in adverse impacts related to corporate governance, workers, human rights, the environment, bribery, and consumers. In the context of cocoa, adverse impacts may relate to child labour, forced labour and human trafficking, deforestation concerns, challenges related to poverty and decent wages, benefits and working conditions in cocoa processing or transportation.

Whereas many companies may understand "risk" primarily as risks to the enterprise – financial risk, market risk, operational risk, reputational risk, etc. the OECD recommendations on responsible business conduct, rather refer to the likelihood of adverse impacts on *people, the environment and society* that enterprises may cause, contribute to, or to which they are directly linked to. In other words, it is an outward-facing approach to risk.

Source: OECD (2018[3]), *OECD Due Diligence Guidance for Responsible Business Conduct*, http://mneguidelines.oecd.org/OECD-Due-Diligence-Guidance-for-Responsible-Business-Conduct.pdf

Understanding the responsibility of an enterprise with regards to adverse impacts

An enterprise can either *cause* adverse impacts, *contribute* to them, or be *directly linked to* them through its business relationships. Depending on the enterprise's involvement with the adverse impacts, actions to address them may vary, from ceasing the actions which are causing or contributing to the impact or using leverage to mitigate or to influence the entity causing or contributing to the adverse impact (see Figure 5).

Understanding the enterprise's relationship to adverse impacts such as child labour and forced labour is key to designing and implementing its response to them. Companies are encouraged to supplement their knowledge on the relationship to an adverse impact by referring to the OECD Due Diligence Guidance for further detail on what is meant by cause, contribute to and directly linked to adverse impacts.

Figure 5. Addressing potential and actual adverse impacts

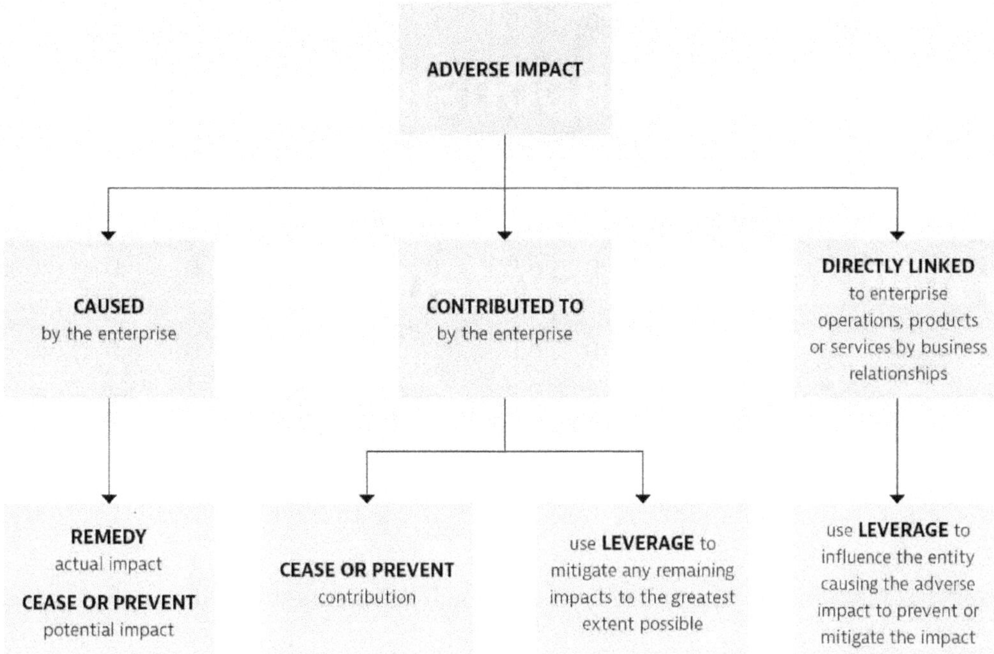

Source: OECD (2018[3]), *OECD Due Diligence Guidance for Responsible Business Conduct*, http://mneguidelines.oecd.org/OECD-Due-Diligence-Guidance-for-Responsible-Business-Conduct.pdf

Table 1 provides examples to illustrate what this relationship to the harm can mean for companies operating in the cocoa sector in relation to child labour and forced labour issues.

Table 1. Examples to help define company relationship with child labour and forced labour impacts

Business is...	Examples in the cocoa sector
Causing (or would cause) an adverse impact if the enterprise's activities on their own are sufficient to result in the adverse impact.	• A business is directly employing children below the minimum working age specified in national legislation (or the ILO Convention No. 138), or is using any individual under the age of 18 to undertake hazardous activities (e.g. land clearing, exposure to hazardous agro-chemicals, sharp tools, carrying heavy loads etc.).
Contributing to (or would contribute to) an impact if its activities, in combination with the activities of other entities cause the impact, or if the activities of the enterprise cause, facilitate or incentivise another entity to cause an adverse impact. Contribution must be substantial, meaning that it does not include minor or trivial contributions.	• A cocoa trader is a long-term, primary buyer of cocoa from a co-operative known to rely heavily on the use of child labour. If the trader continues buying cocoa from the co-operative over time without any attempts to use its leverage to prevent or mitigate the child labour, it may be considered to be contributing to child labour.
Being directly linked to (or would be directly linked to) an adverse impact through the "linkage" between the adverse impact and the enterprise's products, services or operations through another entity (i.e. business relationship).	• A pension group invests in a fund that in turn invests in a co-operative where child labour has been found. The pension fund is directly linked to adverse human rights impacts. • A cocoa trader buys from a smallholder farm that withholds the wages of their workers during the harvest period. As a result, workers are unable to leave their employment. • A chocolate confectionary business buys from a co-operative where child labour has been found.

Source: OECD/FAO (2016[2]), OECD-FAO Guidance for Responsible Agricultural Supply Chains, https://doi.org/10.1787/9789264251052-en; ILO/IOE (2015[5]), How to do business with respect for children's right to be free from child labour: ILO-IOE child labour guidance tool for business, https://www.ilo.org/ipec/Informationresources/WCMS_IPEC_PUB_27555/lang-en/index.htm

Step 1: Embed responsible business conduct and due diligence into policies and management systems

Step 1 of the OECD due diligence framework is about having robust policies and corporate management systems in place. This chapter outlines what this means for companies undertaking due diligence in cocoa supply chains in relation to human rights impacts, such as child labour and forced labour.

Strategic questions for enterprises to ask

- Does your company have a public policy document in which it commits to respecting internationally recognised human rights, including children rights, and the right to be free from forced labour?
- Does this policy reference relevant international standards from the ILO relating to child labour and forced labour and make a commitment to carry out due diligence, using the OECD approach?
- Has this policy been approved at the most senior level of your company and is it clear who is responsible for overseeing the implementation of this policy?
- Have you established a system of controls and transparency along the cocoa supply chain? This could be a chain of custody system (e.g. using documents) or a traceability scheme, or the identification of upstream actors in the cocoa supply chain.
- Do your suppliers understand how to comply with your company policy on human rights, including child labour and forced labour issues? Is it incorporated into supplier contracts or written agreements?
- Is there a system for collecting and reacting to grievances/issues pertaining to child labour and forced labour raised by staff, business partners, and local communities and others?

Embed responsible business conduct due diligence into policies and management systems

Establish and/or update policies with clear references to child labour and forced labour

- Corporate policies should reflect your company's commitment to address child labour and forced labour, respecting child rights in line with national and international standards (e.g. ILO) as well as the OECD recommendations on risk-based due diligence. While child labour and forced labour are recognised as human rights issues in the cocoa sector, policies may also include other human rights concerns, such as freedom of association, gender equality, worker health and safety, tenure rights, access to land as well as the sustainable use of natural resources (land and water) and the protection of forests and biodiversity (OECD/FAO, 2016[2]).
- Companies are encouraged to state that the policy is valid throughout the entire supply chain including at the farm level.
- Standards should apply equally to all people.
- Policies should be approved at the most senior level of the company and be reviewed regularly to reflect new risks in the enterprise's cocoa operations, supply chain and other business relationships. For example, policies may be updated to reflect changes to sourcing areas, new human rights risks in the cocoa supply chain, and evolving international standards and national legislation.[6]
- Policies may include a commitment to work with farmers and their communities, governments, civil society and other relevant stakeholders to collectively address the root causes of child labour and forced labour.

Structure internal management systems and human resources to support due diligence

Based on policies developed, internal management systems and human resources can further support due diligence through additional actions, such as:

- Define management commitment and secure budget to train staff and develop a programme to address human rights risks and impacts such as child labour and forced labour
- Strengthen supplier and SME capacity to conduct effective due diligence to address human rights risks and impacts, including child labour and forced labour
- Train staff on issues of child labour and forced labour, making sure that they understand the complexities of how to best address these adverse impacts

Establish a system of controls and transparency along the supply chain

To adequately identify and address actual and potential adverse human rights impacts such as child labour and forced labour in the supply chain, the OECD recommends that companies (upstream and downstream) establish a system of controls and transparency over the supply chain. Establishing such a system depends on where companies operate in the supply chain and how much visibility and control they have over the supply chain.

Establishing a system of controls can be done through a chain of custody approach (which is document driven, such as through keeping records of the age of workers), or a traceability/certification system. Such systems, and how they are embedded into the company's management systems, should be explained in the company's policy. It should be noted that industry certification schemes may help support a company's due diligence but should not replace a company's due diligence. Individual responsibility for due diligence remains with the company.

Make the policy publicly available and communicate it to all personnel, suppliers, business partners and relevant stakeholders

The policy should be communicated widely to employees and business partners such as farmers, traders or processors, exporters and importers of cocoa beans. Relevant additional stakeholders may include industry or multi-stakeholder initiatives, national/regional governments in producing countries, local NGOs, and community-based organisations. Companies are encouraged to:

- Ensure that personnel and suppliers in your cocoa supply chain have a baseline understanding of human rights, especially of child labour and forced labour issues, as well as the sector and issue-specific indicators that can be used to assess those risks and impacts in the supply chain, and how to alert management if such adverse impacts are found.
- Build the commercial business case for the policy, clarifying departments' specific responsibilities and tying actions to legal requirements and customer demands. Assign responsibility for implementing the policies across relevant departments, for example legal, procurement, stakeholder engagement, supplier engagement and public affairs, among others.
- Develop, communicate and maintain an internal reporting structure within your company at key junctures. Cross-functional groups can share information and decision-making about risks and actual impacts and the progress of your company's due diligence activities in the cocoa supply chain.

Incorporate due diligence expectations into supplier contracts or written agreements

- Include provisions on child labour and forced labour and any other relevant human rights risks in supplier contracts, supplier codes of conduct or other forms of written agreements. Company expectations, including contractual obligations with defined penalties for breaches, should be clearly communicated. Policy materials should be translated and provided to suppliers and business relationships in their own language.

- Communicate the expectation on suppliers to cascade your company's policies through the supply chain and to establish a system of controls and transparency. Supplier or vendor summits can communicate your company's due diligence requirements and showcase better performing peers to promote learning.
- Where a company sources from a supplier where child labour or forced labour are a risk, consider including contractual language to undertake unannounced visits of suppliers' activities or require them to participate in the business' system of controls.
- Train suppliers – especially SMEs – to operationalise risk-based due diligence to address adverse impacts especially child labour and forced labour. This could include, for example the promotion of this Handbook amongst suppliers, developing a standardised reporting framework on risks and actual impacts, sharing examples of suppliers' policies on child labour and forced labour, and helping them strengthen assessment systems to ensure compliance such as age verification systems.
- Work with suppliers to address barriers to the implementation of due diligence, for example, by increasing the percentage of directly sourced cocoa and engaging with national traceability systems to improve visibility where cocoa is sourced from middlemen and traders.

Box 3. Considerations for SMEs

- Consult with local employer associations, industry or multi-stakeholder initiatives when developing policies on due diligence as they may have good practice examples that can be drawn upon. Many of these materials are publicly available.
- Work with peers and organisations in the cocoa sector that can help engage stakeholders on the ground or internationally or support trainings of staff and suppliers on due diligence and in particular addressing child labour and forced labour risks.
- Check publicly available resources from international organisations such as the OECD, ILO, United Nations Children's Fund (UNICEF) and Food and Agriculture Organization of the United Nations (FAO) on child labour for business and what companies can do to address these risks.
- Appoint someone responsible for human rights, even if not in a full-time role. Simpler hierarchies and less siloed structures can provide an advantage for smaller business, including cross-functional co-ordination and more direct involvement of senior decision-makers.

Step 2: Identify, assess and prioritise child labour and forced labour risks in the supply chain

In line with Step 2 of the OECD due diligence framework, this chapter explains how companies can develop a complete picture of their cocoa supply chain to identify, assess and prioritise potential and actual adverse human rights impacts such as child labour and forced labour.

Strategic questions for enterprises to ask

- Have you mapped your cocoa supply chain to identify your key business relationships?
- Do you have a clear understanding of the conditions under which your cocoa beans/ground beans have been harvested, processed and transported?
- Have you reviewed the risk management practices of suppliers in the cocoa supply chain at risk for child labour and forced labour?
  - For **manufacturers, brands, retailers (and in some cases processors)**: Have you identified the "control points" in the cocoa supply chain? Are you able to engage with these control points to verify that they are conducting due diligence in according to OECD recommendations?
  - For **processors (when applicable), traders, distributors, transporters, farms and co-operatives:** Do you know where your cocoa beans and raw materials are coming from – for example which countries, which farms, which intermediary enterprises beyond your immediate suppliers?
- Following risk identification, is risk assessment and prioritisation of adverse impacts on human rights being done based on likelihood and severity rather than those that are easiest to fix?
- Has your company engaged with relevant stakeholders to understand the local context and stakeholders' role in identifying and assessing human rights risks, including child labour and forced labour?

Identify and assess actual and potential adverse human rights impacts associated with the enterprise's operations, products or services

Map the supply chain

Companies should conduct a high-level mapping of the supply chain and systematically work towards a fuller picture. A high-level mapping requires identifying the various actors involved, including when relevant the names of immediate suppliers and business partners and the sites of operations.

Mapping can be complemented with data and information from certification and traceability schemes, company certifications, public summaries of audit reports and records of visits to cocoa production, transformation or storage sites. The extent of information collected by enterprises on business partners depends on the severity of the risks (in the case of child labour and forced labour risks this would be high) and how closely linked the enterprise is to the identified risk.

Upstream versus downstream: The OECD recommendations for supply chain due diligence generally group companies operating along supply chains into upstream and downstream companies. In the agriculture sector, companies in the production sector are considered upstream companies. As highlighted earlier, this covers farmers, including small to large family farms, farmer organisations, co-operatives and private enterprises, as well as companies that invest in land and directly manage farms or plantations. All other companies – i.e. wholesalers, traders, transportation companies, manufacturers of food, feed and beverages, textile and biofuel producers and retailers and supermarkets are considered companies in the downstream segment of the supply chain.[7] Such a differentiation might not strictly apply to all companies in the cocoa sector. While farmers and co-operatives are generally considered as upstream actors, and manufacturers, brands and retailers as downstream actors, processors (refiners and grinders), traders, distributors and transporters could at times be allocated to either one of these categories depending on their business model and where they operate. In this Handbook, we have listed the specific types of companies to which a recommendation applies to.

Downstream companies (such as manufacturers, brands and retailers and in some cases processors), that are several tiers removed from the source of cocoa production may not be able to map all their suppliers and business partners initially. To do so may require working through the tier-1 and sub-tier suppliers, as well as with multi-stakeholder or industry initiatives. Downstream companies should systematically work towards a complete picture of their business relationships over time, prioritising cocoa coming from countries, regions and communities that are at the highest risk of child labour and/or forced labour.

- **Farms and co-operatives** should be able to provide the name of the producer unit and/or co-operative; address and site identification; contact details of the site manager; cocoa quantity, dates and methods of production; number of workers by age and gender; list of risk management practices; transportation routes; and risk assessments that have been undertaken.
- **Processors, transporters, traders and distributors** could request the above information from producers while documenting similar information for their own operations. Where information is not available, efforts should be undertaken to collect it in collaboration with the farms and co-operatives. Verification of information should be undertaken through on-site visits where possible. Several large cocoa traders use Global Positioning System (GPS) technology to identify farms and co-operatives co-ordinates in higher-risk countries. Once mapping is complete, this information can be used to help to identify more particular risk factors for child labour and forced labour, as well as other salient risks such as deforestation, at the regional and community level.
- **Manufacturers, brands and retailers** should find out what information exists and is shared from their upstream business partners and incorporate this information into their supply chain mapping. Downstream companies are expected to identify and work with businesses operating at control points (also known as choke points) of the supply chain to verify that these entities are conducting due diligence in accordance with OECD recommendations.

Control points are businesses operating at key transformation points in the supply chain, such as processing, who have greater visibility and leverage over suppliers upstream in the supply chain.[8] Control points are typically situated in the part of the supply chain with relatively few actors, that process a majority of a given commodity, and have a good level of visibility over the circumstances of production and trade of the upstream supply chain. Control points in the cocoa supply chain could include, for example, traders, grinders and cocoa exporters or importers.

Identify risks and impacts in each part of the supply chain

Once the supply chain is mapped, companies should identify the main human rights risks and impacts along the supply chain. Figure 6 provides a simplified schema of the cocoa supply chain and points in the chain where human rights risks, including that of child labour and forced labour, can typically be found.

This step of due diligence can be conducted using reports on the cocoa sector and supply chain, information from suppliers and industry associations, multi-stakeholder initiatives, investigative reports from NGOs and international organisations focused on child labour and forced labour impacts, as well as a company's own research on the sector and prevalent human rights issues.

Figure 6. Human rights risks across the cocoa supply chain

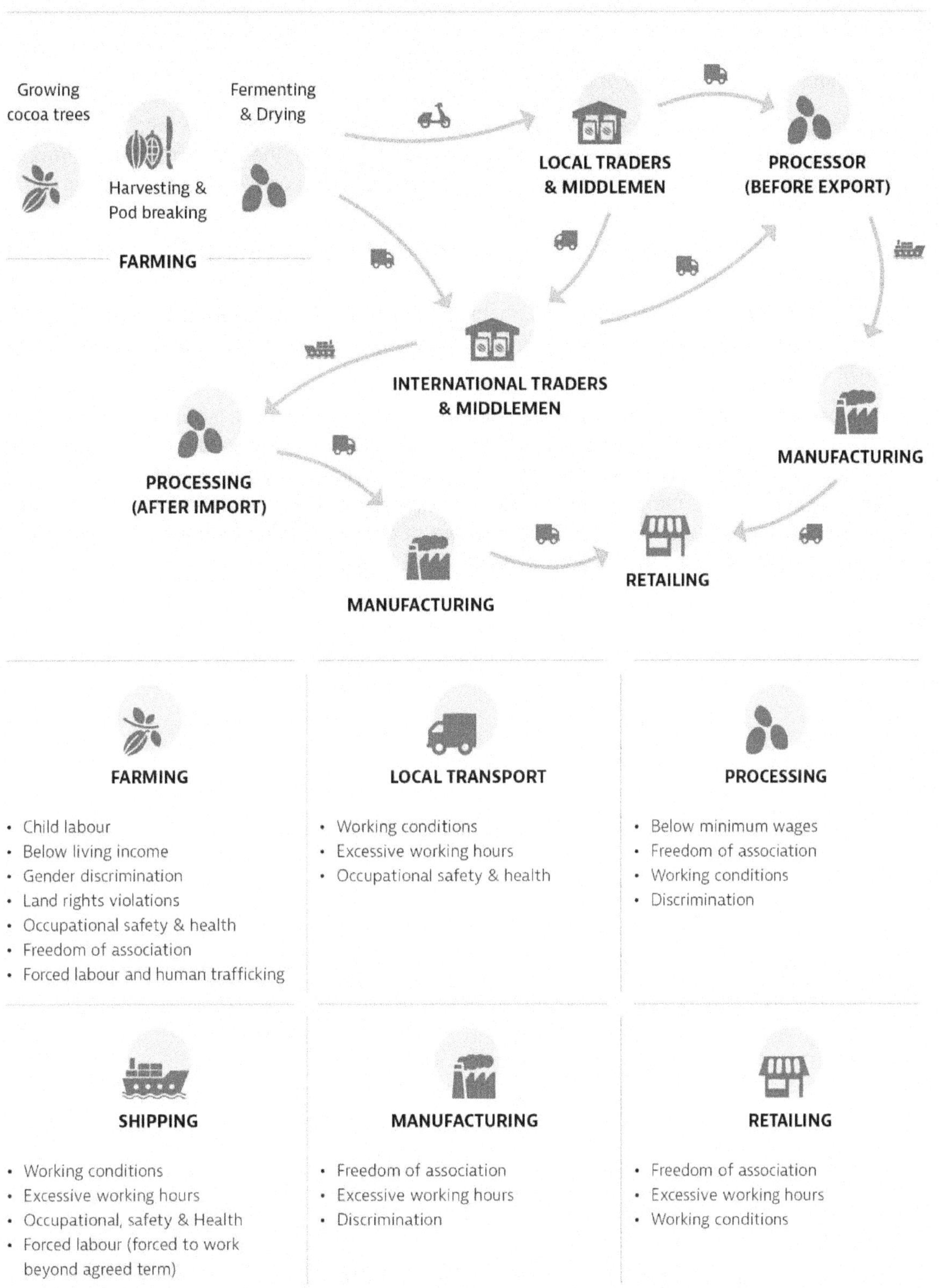

Source: Adapted from UNICEF (2018[23]), Children's Rights in the Cocoa-Growing Communities of Côte d'Ivoire: Synthesis Report, https://sites.unicef.org/csr/css/synthesis-report-children-rights-cocoa-communities-en.pdf; ICI (2020[24]), Cocoa Barometer 2020, https://www.cocoainitiative.org/knowledge-hub/resources/2020-cocoa-barometer.

Assess child labour and forced labour risks and impacts in cocoa supply chains

Once the overall risks and impacts along the supply chain are identified, companies can undertake a more detailed assessment of child labour and forced labour risks and impacts.

When completing a risk assessment, it is important to:

- Regularly review each stage of production and trade, and consider new and emerging trends, including drivers of child labour and forced labour in the region, the type and size of farms as well as the policy, legal, economic, social or contextual causes that can lead to child labour and forced labour.
- Collaborate with local authorities and stakeholders on the ground to support risk assessment and farm level monitoring.
- Put in place systems such as Child Labour Monitoring and Remediation Systems (CLMRS), to prevent, identify and address child labour and forced labour and report on results to the designated senior management.

Companies operating in the cocoa sector will most likely have identified child labour and forced labour as severe human rights issues at the farming level. CLMRS is a tool that can help identify and assess risks in more detail (in addition to providing prevention and remediation support). CLMRS are built around community facilitators (often farmers themselves) who are connected to cocoa-farming co-operatives. They visit households, raise awareness on the dangers of child labour, and identify children engaged in hazardous work. Box 4 provides more information about CLMRS.

Box 4. Where do Child Labour Monitoring and Remediation Systems (CLMRS) fit into risk-based due diligence?

CLMRS can be a way to undertake human rights due diligence in relation to child labour. The concept was initially developed by the ILO to monitor child labour in a wide variety of geographic contexts and across supply chains. In 2012, ICI adapted the CLMRS to the cocoa sector and today, CLMRS are used by many companies.

A recent benchmarking study defines that any effective CLMRS (ICI, 2021[25]) should be able to perform four core functions:

- Raise awareness on child labour and resulting harm amongst farmers, children and members of the wider community
- Identify children in child labour through an active monitoring process, using standardised data collection tools
- Provide prevention and remediation support to children in child labour, and others at risk, and document the support provided
- Follow-up with children identified in child labour to monitor their status on a regular basis until they have stopped engaging in child labour.

Figure 7. ICI's Child Labour Monitoring and Remediation Systems (CLMRS)

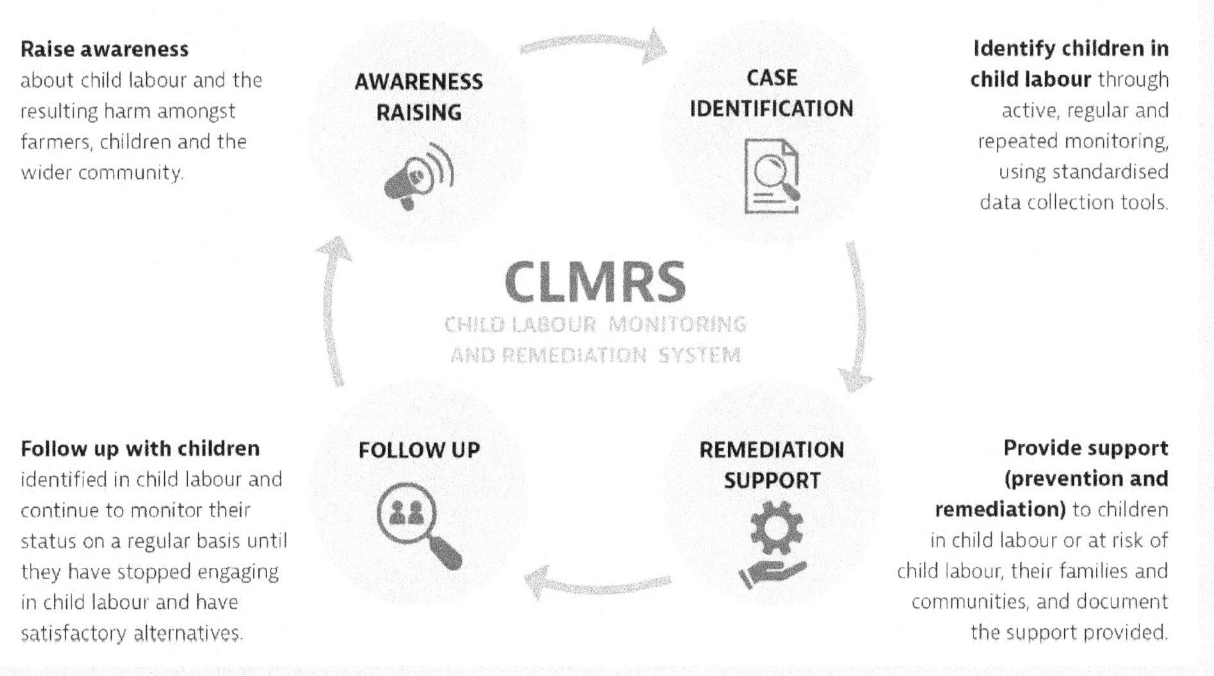

Note: For further details, see section on *Reaching scale and impact to address child labour and forced labour through collaboration*: Provide for or co-operate in remediation when appropriate.
Source: Adapted from ICI (n.d.[26]), Child Labour Monitoring and Remediation Systems: Introduction, https://clmrs.cocoainitiative.org/introduction

Resources to help companies assess risks and impacts of child labour and forced labour

There are a number of useful resources available to help companies assess the risk and impacts of child labour and forced labour. Table 2 can be used as a guide to help businesses assess the level of risk of child labour and forced labour associated with specific indicators.

Table 2. Considerations and risk indicators for assessing child labour and forced labour in cocoa sourcing

Consideration	Indicators	Suggested Questions	Data Sources
Development Context of the Country or Region related to Cocoa Sourcing	**Economic** • High poverty and unemployment rates; high presence of informal labour sector • Minimum wage for agricultural workers (including in the cocoa sector) is not met, or inadequate • Existence of climate-related risks which may lead to lower productivity on farms, impacting revenue and leading to lower income levels (poverty) **Social and Contextual** • Characteristics of gender inequality as an entrenched social norm • Presence and characteristics of ethnic, religious based discrimination • Percentage of children completing secondary school versus children out of school • Presence and quality of free public schooling. Issues which may affect access (for example, for uniforms, equipment, stationary, teacher salary supplements, boarding fees, etc.), informal fees (for example bribes), violence in schools, lack of water and sanitation facilities, cultural norms, and gender discrimination • Level of farmer organisation; and prevalence of functional and effective cocoa co-operatives representing and supporting farmers • Labour characteristics: availability of adult labour, use of daily or seasonal workers, presence of migrant workers	• Which countries does the company source from? Is the minimum wage met in each country? If available, what is the expected living wage for each country? • Is smallholder farming a key part of the economy? • How operational are co-operatives and farmer registration systems – are they representative and effective in giving farmers voice? • Within those countries, which are the highest risk regions and districts for child labour and forced labour?	• UNDP Human Development Index • UNICEF country statistics • Children's Rights and Business Atlas • World Bank Country Profiles • IFC GMAP Database (the global map of environmental and social risks in agro-commodity production) • ILO-IPEC country dashboard database • FAO Family Farming Knowledge Platform • Cocoa Barometer • US Department of State Human Rights Reports, and reports on child labour and forced labour (countries and list of goods) • Walk Free's Global Slavery Index • National databases from local Ministry of Agriculture, Ministry of Employment or Ministry of Education • IOM migration data portal • The Living Income Community of Practice by GIZ/ISEAL/Sustainable Food Lab
International Framework (Legal and Policy Framework)	• Adoption of key international frameworks and ratifications of international conventions	• Are international and regional instruments related to forced labour ratified? • Are international and regional instruments related to child labour ratified?	• ILO Information System on International Labour Standards (NORMLEX) • ILO Forced Labour Observatory database • Children's Rights and Business Atlas
National Regulatory Environment (Legal and Policy Framework)	• National regulatory environment • Strength of government institutions and enforcement mechanisms with regards to child labour and forced labour • Availability of social services • Existence of freedom of association and collective bargaining rights in labour legislation • Existence of robust labour migration governance	• What does national law say about child labour, specifically in relation to sectors and ages? Is it the same for all genders? • What tasks are defined as hazardous work for children in the country? • What does the national law say about forced labour and human trafficking?	• ILO-IPEC country dashboard database • ILO Forced Labour Observatory database • Alliance 8.7 Pathfinder Country Progress Reports on Forced Labour and Child Labour • US Department of Labour reports on child labour and

Consideration	Indicators	Suggested Questions	Data Sources
	• Existence of robust land tenure rights, which consider special needs of women, migrants, and others • Existence of safeguards and protections for indigenous rights, ethnic and/or religious minorities' rights • Regulations or policy frameworks such as National Action Plans on Business and Human Rights and/or human rights due diligence; with support for business to implement responsible business conduct	• Is there a gap between national and international standards on child labour? • Is there a gap between national and international standards on forced labour? • How is the law on child labour enforced in the country? Is there a National Action Plan to address child labour? Or is the country an Alliance 8.7 Pathfinder country? • How is the law on freedom of association and collective bargaining enforced in the country? • How is the law on forced labour and human trafficking enforced in the country? Is there a National Action Plan to address it? • Is there a reliable and sustainable mechanism to monitor child labour in the country? Is it cross-sector? • Is there a reliable and sustainable mechanism to treat labour-related grievances in the country? Is it functional, i.e. were grievances received in the past 12 months and were they addressed?	forced labour, which include information about enforcement, inter-agency mechanisms. • UNICEF country statistics • Children's Rights and Business Atlas • National legislation, National Action Plans on Business and Human Rights, National Action Plans on child labour, government databases • International Cocoa Initiative Knowledge Hub • Interviews with local civil society organisations and government authorities
Child Labour Specific Risk Indicators	Prevalence data on child labour is the best indicator of the likelihood of child labour. Where data on child labour prevalence is unavailable or not specific to the region, farmer group, or community, factors known to be correlated with higher child labour prevalence can help identify where risks may be higher. **At community level:** • Limited access to quality education (including low levels of educational attainment, high student to teacher ratios, teacher absence, teacher violence, lack of school food, lack of school toilets) • Limited access to water, sanitation, electricity and health care • Low levels of women's empowerment • Absence of farmer organisations such as co-operatives. • Limited access to adult labour • Accessibility of cocoa production areas **At household level:** • Age and sex of children in the household • Plot size and production volumes • Household income • Children's school attendance	• How prevalent is child labour? • Is accurate data on farming households available? • Is formal education/schooling accessible? • What is the level of women's empowerment in the community; are they involved in decision making at community level, and are vulnerable women including female headed households supported? • Are there farming co-operatives that can work with farmers in the community? Do they implement effective measures to prevent and address child labour?	• Surveys of child labour prevalence (e.g. The NORC cocoa report) • Data collected from CLMRS • Co-operative registers of farming households • Community assessment tools (e.g. ICI's protective community index, or child labour risk calculator tools) • Interviews with local co-operatives, civil society organisations, government authorities, local school staff, religious and community organisations, such as local child protection networks, or women's empowerment committees

Source: ICI (2019[27]), Using community-level data to understand child labour risk in cocoa-growing areas of Côte d'Ivoire and Ghana: Executive summary, https://www.cocoainitiative.org/knowledge-hub/resources/using-community-level-data-understand-child-labour-risk-infographic; ICI (n.d.[28]), Protective Community Index, https://www.cocoainitiative.org/knowledge-hub/resources/protective-community-index; ICI (n.d.[29]), Community Child Labour Risk Assessment – Data Collections Tools, https://www.cocoainitiative.org/knowledge-hub/resources/community-child-labour-risk-assessment-data-collections-tools; Sadhu (2020[9]), Assessing Progress in Reducing Child Labor in Cocoa Growing Areas of Côte d'Ivoire and Ghana, https://www.norc.org/PDFs/Cocoa%20Report/NORC%202020%20Cocoa%20Report_English.pdf.

Identifying and assessing forced labour can be challenging since many forms of coercion and exploitation are hidden. Within the cocoa sector, victims may also be located in isolated areas and inaccessible to community monitors. ICI and Verité have worked together to examine how the ILO forced labour indicators can be used to identify cases of forced labour in the cocoa sector. Table 3 can be used as a guide to help businesses assess the level of risk associated with the different indicators. As a general rule, the presence of one indicator under "involuntariness" ***and*** one indicator under "menace of penalty" requires immediate action. Preventative action is recommended if at least one indicator exists under ***either*** "involuntariness" or "menace of penalty". The second table shows common indicators for both "involuntariness" and "menace of penalty" in the cocoa sector.

Table 3. Operational-level forced labour indicators

Indicator of involuntariness	Indicator of penalty / menace of penalty	Forced labour	Observation
At least one	**At least one**	Yes	Red case Action required
At least one indicator	None	At risk	Orange case Preventive action recommended
None	**At least one indicator**	At risk	Orange case Preventive action recommended
None	None	**No**	Green case No action required

Source: Adapted by Verite and ICI, from ILO forced labour indicators.

Table 4. Common indicators for the cocoa sector

Indicators of involuntariness	Indicators of menace of penalty
• Work without the free and informed consent of the worker • Circumstances that may lead to involuntary work, when undertaken under deception or uninformed decisions • Unfree recruitment at birth or through transaction such as slavery or bonded labour • Situations where the worker must perform a job of different nature from that specified during recruitment without a person's consent • Abusive requirements for overtime or on-call work that were not previously agreed with the employer • Work in hazardous conditions to which the worker has not consented, with or without compensation or protective equipment • Work with very low or no wages • Degrading living conditions imposed by the employer, recruiter, or other third-party • Work for other employers than agreed • Work for longer periods of time than agreed • Work with no or limited freedom to terminate work contract • Multiple dependence from employer	• The means of coercion used to impose work on a worker against a person's will • Workers can be subjected to coercion, or verbally threatened by these elements of coercion, or be witness to coercion imposed on other co-workers in relation to involuntary work • Elements of coercion may include, inter alia: o Threats or violence against workers or workers' families and relatives, or close associates o Restrictions on workers' movement o Debt bondage or manipulation of debt o Withholding of wages or other promised benefits o Withholding of valuable documents (such as identity documents or residence permits) o Abuse of workers' vulnerability through the denial of rights or privileges, threats of dismissal or deportation

Box 5. Considerations if you are a...

Farmer and co-operative, trader, distributor, transporter or processor (when applicable):

Mapping the supply chain, identifying and assessing risks and impacts

- Help co-operatives generate and share credible, verifiable, reliable and up-to-date information on the extent of human rights risks and harms, including child labour and forced labour risks. If the data does not exist yet, local staff may be able to collect it, or, if needed, establish a dedicated assessment team to do so.
- Ensure that effective and meaningful consultations with local communities and farmers are held to identify risk, as they are often a good source of information and alerts.
- Use existing supply chain data (including the age and education level of the producer and their children, farm size, number of workers) to establish a risk model.[1]
- Use methodologies such as CLMRS to identify children in and at risk of child labour. Specific vulnerability factors linked to the risk of forced labour of children can also be integrated into CLMRS.
- Share the results of your company's risk assessments with downstream enterprises, especially where these assessments identified risk or impacts of child labour and forced labour.

Manufacturer, brand, retailer and in some cases processor:

Mapping the supply chain

- Work with your first-tier suppliers to get visibility on the source of cocoa, including identifying control points. Establish systems of control further upstream in the supply chain.
- Consistently request and underline the importance of knowing the source of your cocoa and having visibility of the business relationships involved.
- Support upstream companies or organisations who may have less capacity to map their supply chain by investing in building capacity and resources.

Identifying risks and assessing impacts

- Review the due diligence measures put in place by your suppliers or directly assess their operations, for instance, by conducting visits to farms and their communities.
- Seek information on both the suppliers' systems and the volumes of products they are supplying.
- Consider participating in industry-wide schemes and multi-stakeholder initiatives to obtain relevant information and support your own assessments.
- Request documentation from upstream companies, such as evidence that the supply chain has been mapped and farms within the supply chain are identified, evidence of risk assessments and on-the-ground monitoring, and stakeholder engagement reports at the community and farm level.

SME – upstream and downstream

Mapping the supply chain

- Work in collaboration with other businesses, for example, through national cocoa platforms, industry or multi-stakeholder initiatives to increase leverage and demand for systems of control (including chain of custody and/or traceability) and supply chain transparency.
- Engage with credible certification schemes aligned to OECD recommendations on due diligence to build greater transparency in your supply chain.

Identifying risks and assessing impacts

- Make use of the wide range of resources from industry and multi-stakeholder initiatives and government agencies available as these can help provide up-to-date information to assist your company in evaluating risks. There are resources that help SMEs to carry out risk analyses for cocoa-growing countries with which they co-operate.[2]
- Some small chocolate producers buy cocoa directly from the farmers and have a very detailed knowledge of their supply chain. Purchasing cocoa directly from producers can also simplify the process of identifying and assessing risk as farmers have knowledge of the conditions under which the cocoa is grown and harvested.

Notes:
1: To learn more about risk models, visit ICI's website (ICI, 2021[30]).
2: To find more resources, visit German Initiative on Sustainable Cocoa's webpage (SÜDWIND e.V., 2021[31]).

Step 3: Cease, prevent and mitigate child labour and forced labour impacts

Step 3 is about adopting risk management and mitigation measures and implementing a strategy to address risks and impacts. This chapter illustrates how companies can design a fit-for-purpose strategy to prevent and address child labour and forced labour risks and impacts in the cocoa supply chain.

Strategic questions for enterprises to ask

- Is responsibility for addressing child labour and forced labour risks and adverse impacts assigned to a senior level focal point in your company?
- Do you have a process to mitigate risk and impacts in the upstream part of the supply chain, including with suppliers with whom your company has no contractual relationship?
- Does your risk management plan contain key performance indicators (KPIs) and timelines to measure success in responding to child labour, forced labour and other human rights risks and adverse impacts that have been identified and assessed?
- How does your company collaborate with others when seeking to mitigate or address the identified adverse impacts, especially if your company is not operationally present in the sourcing country?
- Has your company allocated suitable internal resources to enable effective responses to address human rights risks and impacts?

Cease, prevent and mitigate adverse impacts

Design and implement a strategy to respond to adverse risks and impacts

Step 3 of due diligence calls for action to address (cease, prevent and mitigate) the identified potential or actual adverse human rights impacts. The actions that a company takes to respond to these risks and impacts depends on whether it has *caused*, *contributed to*, or is *directly linked to* an adverse impact (for more information on this relationship please see Table 1). All companies regardless of their relationship to child labour and forced labour impacts are encouraged to collaborate with governments, NGOs, international organisations and multi-stakeholder initiatives among others in addressing the systemic drivers of child labour and forced labour in supply chains.

General principles companies should consider when responding to child labour or forced labour in their operations or supply chains

- **Always act in the best interests of the child**. Effective company actions with regards to child labour and forced labour will seek the betterment of the child and prevent the child from being pushed into a situation where the child is further penalised. When a child has been identified in or at risk of child labour, manage the case and discuss possible solutions with the child and child's family in partnership with relevant community, supply chain and national structures.
- **Develop safeguarding protections**. Safeguarding includes a company commitment and plan to keep children safe. At its most basic, safeguarding entails the prevention of physical, sexual and emotional abuse and maltreatment by employees and other persons whom the company is responsible for.
- **Disengage responsibly.** Where there are repeated failed attempts to influence and engage an entity in ceasing actions that cause or contribute to child labour or forced labour, companies should consider disengagement. Disengagement should be conducted in a responsible time bound way, ensuring in the first instance that children and their families are supported.

What steps should companies that are causing or contributing to child labour or forced labour take?

In these cases, the first step is to stop the activities that are causing or contributing to child labour or forced labour, before working to prevent and mitigate future adverse impacts. For example, if a company is contributing to child labour or forced labour through its purchasing practices, stopping these activities may mean working with business teams to institute longer-horizon purchasing agreements that provide predictability for co-operatives and farming families. In general, working to prevent and mitigate future child labour or forced labour impacts may include reinforcing policies; building capacity of due diligence systems of suppliers and business partners; establishing or strengthening preventative and mitigation measures such as through CLMRS; ensuring regular training of staff (including field staff, buyers and extension agents that are promoting crop production in addition to those responsible for labour monitoring) and verifying suppliers' due diligence systems.

Specific examples of steps that can be taken in the case of child labour and forced labour can be found below, and practical examples of measures to prevent and mitigate adverse impacts can be found in the section "Adopt risk prevention and mitigation mechanisms".

Child labour:

- When potential or actual cases of child labour have been identified as being caused, or contributed to, by the company, tailored support should be provided. This could for example be a referral to the appropriate local child protection authority or community-based organisation. For companies to know how to prioritise which children should receive support, a decision-tree methodology with specific time bound actions, such as that developed by ICI can be applied to guide decision-making (see Figure 8).
- Companies should discuss possible solutions with the child and their family, in partnership with relevant community structures, authorities and law enforcement services (when necessary). Companies without a system in place are encouraged to develop one by forming partnerships with civil society, government social workers or community child protection structures. Child protection systems should build on government standard operational procedures (SOPs). For example, in Ghana there are Inter-Sectoral SOPs for Child Protection and Family Welfare.[1]
- For children above the minimum legal working age according to national laws and who have finished compulsory schooling, companies can consider engaging them in safe work. This includes but is not limited to non-hazardous positions suitable for young workers, ensuring hazardous positions are off-limits to young workers or rendering them non-hazardous. This may be a practical approach for working age children who are under 18 years of age.

Forced labour:

Forced labour requires an immediate response from companies. Due to its severe nature, cases of forced labour must be reported to the authorities.

- Law enforcement, local authorities and protection agencies may be able to help identify the individual needs of the victim(s), and services needed. Referrals should be based on a strong understanding of the national mechanisms and pathways for remediation available in a country. Where victim services are not available through public officials, companies may consider engaging a qualified service provider to undertake remediation of forced labour situations.
- When a situation of forced labour is identified, first ensure the immediate safety of the child/victim. This includes putting appropriate child/victim safeguarding protections in place. At its most basic, safeguarding entails the prevention of physical, sexual and emotional abuse and maltreatment by employees and other persons whom the company is responsible for.
- Companies can discuss possible solutions with the victim (e.g. paying back owed wages, services to find alternative employment), in partnership with relevant community structures, authorities and law enforcement services, when necessary.

What steps should companies that are directly linked to child labour or forced labour through a business relationship take?

For companies that are directly linked to child labour or forced labour through a business relationship, it is important to influence the business partner that is causing or contributing to child and forced labour to take measures to end these adverse impacts. For example, companies can work with business partners to ensure that children are removed from child labour and a time-bound plan is put in place to help the child access education, rehabilitation, social integration and/or collaborate inactions to support the needs of their family.

- Build leverage to influence through consultation with the victim, relevant community, supply-chain and national structures.
- Participate in industry or multi-stakeholder initiatives to increase leverage if entities are taking insufficient action.
- Work with the business partner causing child labour and forced labour impacts to provide remedy to victims (see the following sections Remedy: Provide for or co-operate in remediation when appropriate and Reaching scale and impact to address child labour and forced labour through collaboration).
- Consider discontinuing engagement with business partners if nothing is done (over a given period) to address these impacts and prevent future incidences from occurring. If engagement efforts fail to result in changes within a time bound period, companies should responsibly disengage from doing business with these business partners.

How can companies use leverage to influence the behaviour of companies causing or contributing to child labour or forced labour?

Leverage exists "where the enterprise has the ability to effect change in the wrongful practices of the entity that causes the harm" (OECD, 2011[32]). Enterprises often have more leverage than they realise.

This can include, for example (ILO/IOE, 2015[5]):

- Traditional commercial leverage: Include expectations around preventing and addressing child labour, forced labour and respect for human rights in commercial contracts
- Broader business leverage: Support upstream supply partners through capacity building, awareness raising, and sharing tools and resources such as this Handbook
- Leverage together with business peers: Create collective action with other companies sourcing from the same area at risk for child labour and/or forced labour. This may include companies outside the agriculture or cocoa sector
- Leverage through bilateral engagement: Engage one-on-one with one or more other actors, such as governments, business peers, trade unions, international organisations or civil society organisations
- Leverage through industry/multi-stakeholder collaboration: Collaborate with governments, business peers, trade unions, international organisations, civil society organisations and/or multi-stakeholder initiatives.

If leverage and influence fail to result in an improvement on addressing child labour and forced labour, ending the business relationship may be appropriate. In cases of disengagement, care should be taken that children, farmers and workers are not pushed into worse situations. Companies should avoid placing the burden of compliance on business entities in the supply chain with the least capacity and should rather support investment in systems and support measures for these businesses to change behaviour.

Figure 8. How to prioritise which children receive support in a cocoa farming community?

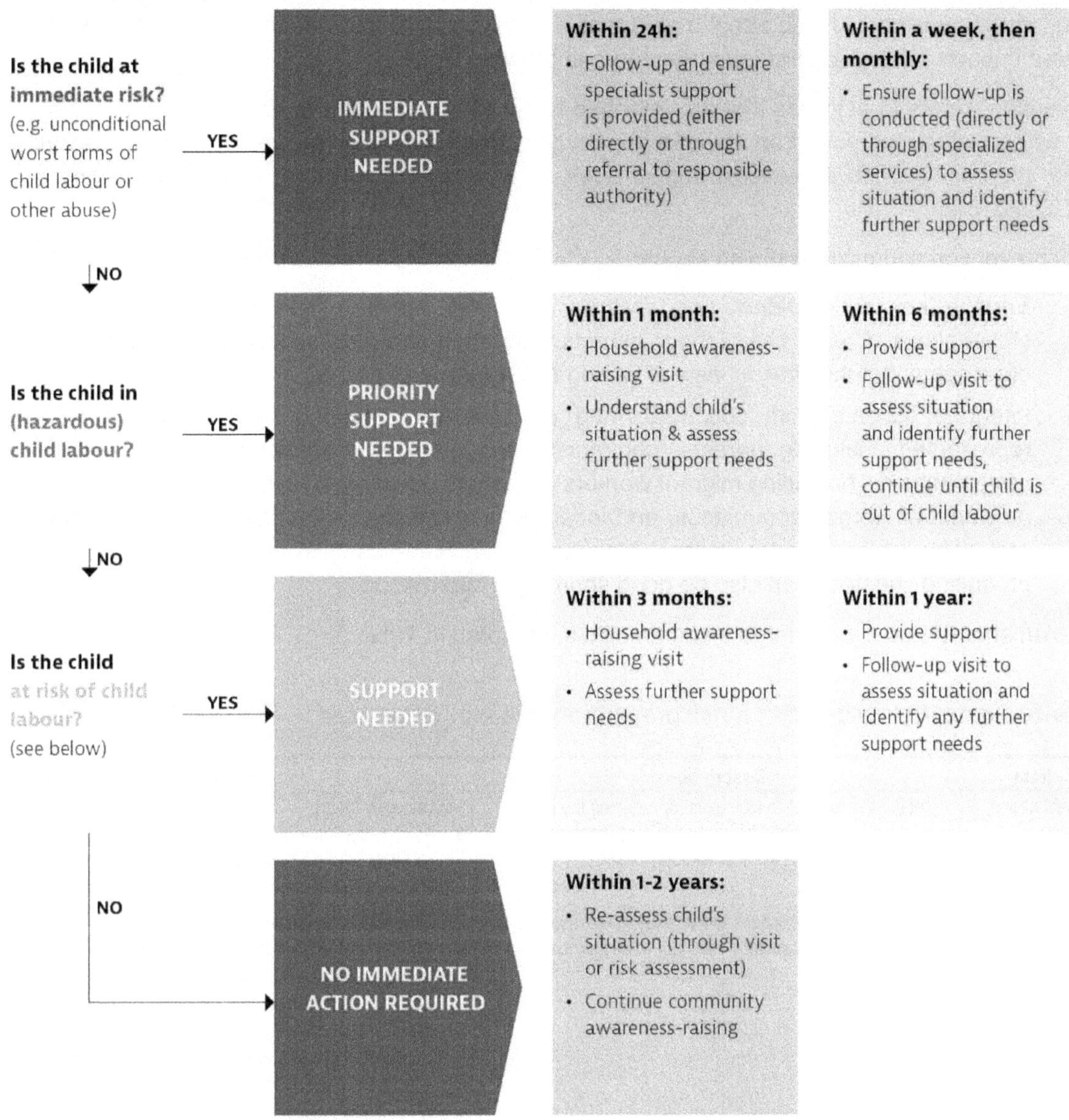

Which children may be at risk of child labour?

Children not in child labour but falling into one of the following groups should be considered at-risk of child labour and prioritised for preventative support:[1]

- Does not attend school/ is often absent
- Lives away from biological parents
- Lives in a single-parent headed household
- Lives in a child-headed household
- Lives in a household where the head of household is illiterate
- Lives in a community with no primary school
- Has a sibling in child labour
- Is a parent themselves

[1] Access to education is fundamental children's right; all other factors have been shown to be correlated with higher likelihood that children engage in hazardous child labour in cocoa.

Source: ICI (2022[33]), *Decision tree: Selecting support to prevent and remediate child labour through a CLMRS*, https://www.cocoainitiative.org/knowledge-hub/resources/selecting-support-prevent-and-remediate-child-labour-through-clmrs.

Adopt risk prevention and mitigation measures

In addition to stopping activities if a company is causing or contributing to child labour or forced labour or influencing the actions of business partners who are causing or contributing to child labour and forced labour, companies should also adopt a plan that is fit for purpose to prevent and mitigate potential future adverse impacts related to child labour and forced labour.

"Prevention" refers to activities that are intended to avoid an adverse impact occurring in the first place (e.g. which reduce the risk of an adverse impact occurring); whereas "mitigation" refers to activities that reduce the impact when an adverse impact does occur. Prevention is the primary goal of due diligence (OECD, 2018[3]).

A risk prevention and mitigation plan should:

- Engage key stakeholders (e.g. children and their families, suppliers, farmers, government stakeholders, CSOs, child labour experts, migration experts, human trafficking experts) in the development of the plan, in view of finding consensus on actions.
- Integrate insights from cocoa growing communities, ensuring both men and women are represented, including parents, community and religious leaders, co-operative staff, worker representatives (including migrant workers), teachers, local organisations such as child protection networks or women committees, and local government authorities that are responsible for child protection, welfare, and education. National Action Plans on child labour and forced labour from producing countries can also be good sources of information.

The plan should also specify targets and timelines, as noted in Table 5.

Table 5. Elements to include in a risk prevention and mitigation plan

Item	Description	Examples
Targets and Timeline	Set targets and define indicators for reducing the risk of child labour and forced labour and other human rights risks and impacts in the cocoa supply chain.	Indicators by [year]: • # of households in cocoa growing communities covered by CLMRS • # of suppliers trained on forced labour prevention
Actions	Devise time bound actions to address the most salient human rights risks such as child labour and forced labour.	To address poverty issues: • Ensure co-operatives have good cash flow by putting a more regular payment plan in place, implement better payment terms, implement the minimum wage and consider how to support living wages • Support access to basic services, including quality education, health, etc.
Resources	Identify resources needed (financial and human) to develop and implement the actions.	• Budget for the actions defined • List of third-party providers active in cocoa growing communities who can help deliver those actions
Roles and responsibilities	Determine who is responsible for implementing the risk management and mitigation measures: • Within the enterprise • Amongst cocoa suppliers • With business partners, both upstream and downstream Relevant personnel must understand the indicators, targets and timelines and their role in implementation.	• Enterprise: Responsible sourcing team is tasked to design the training in co-ordination with the procurement team. • Cocoa Suppliers: Responsible for selecting one representative to participate in the training and incorporating learnings into business practices.
Monitoring and Reporting	Set up monitoring systems for tracking the implementation of the plan and corresponding measures, and the reporting processes to high-level management.	Progress against targets is reviewed at risk management meetings with reporting on key KPIs to senior management, e.g. Responsible Sourcing Director, legal and the CEO

Examples of measures that can be taken to prevent and/or mitigate child labour and forced labour risks and impacts

- **Improve access to quality education** by:
  - Supporting communities to create a good school environment for children by constructing or renovating educational facilities, helping to increase both enrolment and attendance.
  - Running bridging classes to enable out-of-school children to catch up on missed classes,
  - Facilitating access to birth certificates which are necessary for children to attend school in some countries.
- **Support farmer livelihoods**: Poverty and reliance upon cocoa as a single crop are two factors that can place children at higher risk of child labour. Companies can support farmers to diversify their income, which in return can help reduce the vulnerability of farming families to income shocks that can, in some cases, increase the risk for children to work or encourage incidence of forced labour.
- **Promote women's empowerment**: Adult literacy classes, small business or income-generating activities, and Village Savings and Loans Associations (VSLAs) can help address power imbalances between men and women, empowering women which can result in better child protection
- **Establish an effective monitoring and remediation system.** An effective Child Labour Monitoring and Remediation System (CLMRS) can guide companies in providing support to children in child labour, and others at risk and help strengthen company preventative and mitigation measures (see Box 4 for more information on CLMRS).
- **Provide staff training**. Ensure ongoing and refresher training for all staff to ensure violations of child labour and forced labour are prevented. Training should include field staff, buyers and extension agents that are promoting crop production in addition to those responsible for labour monitoring.
- **Consider a landscape approach**. Landscape approaches, which involve all relevant parties in a geographic area, can help by pooling efforts to address child labour and forced labour across stakeholder groups. Some examples of outcomes from landscape approaches are improved access to birth registrations, better living conditions in cocoa growing communities through better access to education and health services, the construction of roads/infrastructure and the establishment of local child protection committees.

Box 6. Considerations for SMEs

- Designate a person in your company to lead your human rights strategy and ensure they have the right training to understand the issues and resources, knowledge and support to implement it, in particular when it comes to child labour and forced labour.
- Consult local employer associations, industry networks, international organisations and multi-stakeholder initiatives to learn how peers and other SMEs are addressing child labour and forced labour risks and impacts in the cocoa sector.
- Include measures to address child labour and forced labour as part of performance reviews and incentives for staff.
- Ensure that your expectations to address both actual and potential adverse impacts of child labour and forced labour identified are included in sales terms, procurement and contracting agreements and practices.
- Share action plans with all your suppliers and ask them to share with sub-suppliers. Enhance co-operation with suppliers identified as being at higher risk for child labour and forced labour.

In addition, upstream SMEs can:

- Design a strategy based on the questions asked by buyers and key affected stakeholders.
- Work with producers, smallholder farmers or other stakeholders in the supply chain, and communicate that strategy downstream.

Source: Adapted from Shift, IEO (2019[34]), SMEs and the Responsibility to Respect Human Rights, https://shiftproject.org/resource/smes-and-the-responsibility-to-respect-human-rights/.

Step 4: Track implementation and results

Step 4 of the OECD due diligence framework is about making sure that your due diligence activities are effective. This chapter describes how companies in the cocoa sector can track the effectiveness of measures implemented to prevent and mitigate human rights risks and impacts such as child labour and forced labour in their supply chains.

Strategic questions for enterprises to ask

- Are you using assessment and grievance data to track the progress of individual suppliers against risk management plans and measures for addressing child labour and forced labour?
- For manufacturers, brands, retailers and in some cases processors, are you verifying that identified control points in the supply chain are conducting due diligence on the upstream portion of the supply chain in accordance with OECD recommendations?
- For farmers and co-operatives, traders, distributors, transporters or processors (when applicable), are you gathering feedback on whether human rights risks and impacts such child labour and forced labour are effectively being addressed?
- Are you tracking cases of child labour and/or forced labour that have been identified and how those cases were handled (i.e. what prevention, mitigation and remediation was provided)?
- Are you tracking progress and impact using appropriate qualitative and quantitative indicators? Those may be aligned with industry monitoring frameworks and government initiatives (e.g. National Action Plans), or developed in consultation with child labour and forced labour experts, trade unions, sector associations or multi-stakeholder initiatives?

Track implementation and results

Tracking and verifying how well due diligence is carried out is instrumental to reducing child labour and forced labour in your supply chain.

Monitor and track implementation and effectiveness of the company's commitments, goals and activities on due diligence

- Assign senior management oversight for ensuring responsibility for tracking and verification of the company's due diligence efforts.
    - A sourcing office within a company may have the primary responsibility for tracking implementation of supplier assessments and corresponding corrective action plans for addressing child labour and forced labour that are time-bound and outcome-oriented.
    - A company's buying department may hold the primary responsibility of tracking rates at which orders are placed late, changed, or cancelled – all practices which may contribute to actual and potential adverse impacts of child labour and forced labour with their suppliers.
    - Operational level staff may seek feedback from impacted stakeholders and rights holders on whether the adverse impacts have been addressed, for example through consulting local communities and authorities, community-based organisations for child protection and women's empowerment, co-operatives and workers' representatives, through collecting feedback from people who attend meetings and forums, or taking note of issues brought to remediation procedures such as child labour and working conditions on cocoa farms.
- Downstream companies should engage with companies and suppliers at control points (e.g. traders, grinders, cocoa importers and exporters) of the cocoa supply chain and assess their due diligence processes and actions.
- Record any children referred to local services in the monitoring system, including the date referred and the date assistance was received. Follow-up with all cases referred to local services, to check

if they received support, understand how their situation has evolved, and identify further support needs.

- In cases of forced labour, companies may be required to publicly disclose them under mandatory disclosure legislation. Cases should be monitored and check-ins done with victims to ensure they receive support and to identify further needs.

What to track and verify?

When looking at what to track and verify, it is useful to consider standardised data collection and how to aggregate data for scale and convergence. One way to do so is to research which indicators and key data points producing country governments, industry or multi-stakeholder initiatives have put in place and to align with them, or to use them directly. National Action Plans (NAPs) and national level child labour survey reports with performance measures (outcome indicators, baseline, targets) can be a useful source.

Table 6. Examples of indicators to track

Examples of child labour indicators	Examples of forced labour indicators
# households and # children covered by a CLMRS or similar programme # cases of child labour identified # children identified in child labour who received support # children identified in child labour who received at least two follow-up visits # children no longer in child labour # households covered by another type of child labour system and impact of these systems	# households reached by awareness-raising on forced labour # households covered by an assessment of forced labour risks # households with access to a grievance mechanism to support forced labour risks and cases # grievances reported in the past 12 months # co-operatives with a forced labour policy in place # people trained on forced labour

Note: Examples of the common child labour indicators agreed on by ICI and the European Platforms on Sustainable Cocoa (ISCOs).

Carry out assessments of the supply chain

- Supply chains are dynamic and can be affected by multiple factors including climate change, epidemics, and other vulnerabilities. Sourcing for cocoa beans can shift quite suddenly changing the risk level involved. Companies need to stay abreast of these changes and adapt their due diligence strategies appropriately. Some companies in the cocoa sector are piloting satellite and LiDAR mapping to provide real-time data and more accurate traceability information, as well as on risks such as deforestation. This helps provide insights into how cocoa is driving deforestation that may also hold a higher risk of forced labour (Myers, 2019[35]).
- Downstream companies should engage suppliers and business partners operating at control points of the supply chain to verify that their risk mitigation measures with regards to child labour and forced labour are up-to-date, and that incidences of child labour and forced labour have been addressed. Establishing a system for regular transfer of information from upstream to downstream enterprises is crucial for promoting transparency in the supply chain over time.

Consult and engage impacted or potentially impacted rightsholders

Stakeholder engagement is an integral part of the OECD due diligence process. Tracking and verification systems are strengthened when they engage stakeholders such as internal staff, representatives of co-operatives and farmers' groups, civil society organisations, workers' representatives, local community leaders and government authorities.

In the context of child labour and forced labour it is important to engage with farmers and farmers' groups, farming families and parents – especially those representing women, civil society organisations working on child labour and forced labour issues, workers' representatives, trade unions and labour leaders, local community leaders, schools, government authorities and agencies including those responsible for child protection and labour rights. These groups should be regularly consulted and engaged to monitor and update information on child labour and forced labour issues.

Downstream companies may wish to work with local and international NGOs experienced in child and labour issues, as well as industry associations and initiatives operating on the ground. Children identified in child labour can be consulted and engaged through household visits, to understand their current situation and work status and monitor any changes, is key. This is a core part of monitoring systems such as CLMRS, which requires regular follow-up visits until a child can be considered "withdrawn" from child labour according to the criteria previously documented.

Conduct periodic reviews of multi-stakeholder and industry initiatives of which the enterprise is a member

The cocoa sector has a number of multi-stakeholder and industry level sustainable cocoa initiatives which can support companies, in particular those companies many tiers removed from the production of cocoa, in conducting due diligence to address child labour and forced labour. These initiatives should be assessed periodically by participating companies as due diligence remains the responsibility of companies themselves. Companies participating or using such initiatives to complement their due diligence actions should check that these initiatives are aligned with OECD recommendations on due diligence.[9]

Include feedback of lessons learned into the enterprise's due diligence to continuously improve the process and outcomes

Companies should undertake a broader assessment of overall due diligence efforts periodically, including through third-party audits by competent and accredited independent parties who are knowledgeable and experienced in child labour and forced labour verification.

Third-party audits are most effective when they are independent, competent and accountable, and conducted in line with OECD recommendations. They should cover, for instance, chain of custody systems, including an evaluation of the quality of documentation, information on child labour and working conditions at the farm level.

Box 7. Considerations if you are a...

Processor (when applicable), trader, distributor, transporter, farm and co-operative:

- Ensure your downstream buyers know how you verify and collect information, including the type of data collected (see Table 6), frequency of collection and who you work with in obtaining that data.
- Be honest in communicating what information you do not have, and why you do not have it.
- Discuss with downstream buyers how they may support your data collection activities, and resources you need. If their leverage is greater than your own, ask for their support to utilise their leverage and capacity.
- Identify and support existing CLMRS and human rights grievance mechanisms and support expansion and coverage.

Manufacturer, brand, retailer (and in some cases processors):

- Organise regular meetings with your suppliers, in particular those operating at control points of the supply (e.g. traders, grinders, cocoa importers and exporters) to assess their due diligence efforts to address child labour and forced labour risks and adverse impacts.
- Identify local NGOs, international organisations with expertise in working on child labour and forced labour cases, and who are knowledgeable of the communities; speak to them regularly to verify that the information you receive from suppliers is accurate.
- Involve local NGOs and/or trade unions to support ongoing monitoring systems on farms.

SMEs

- Upstream SMEs should understand the type and frequency of data needed to fulfil buyer or legal compliance requests. Seek ways in which data can be pooled across customers, or how technology can be used to increase efficiency and get best value for effort.
- Upstream SMEs should incorporate the process of tracking and verifying effectiveness data into existing community-based or supply chain systems, such as the CLMRS. This ensures that feedback from internal and external sources is incorporated into the tracking of the process and helps to address potential financial and/or capacity concerns.
- SMEs, regardless of their position in the supply chain, should consider using tools and standardised indicators from industry or multi-stakeholder initiatives they may be part of. This reduces duplication of efforts while helping pool leverage and resources.
- Robust, long-term processes are needed within a company for tracking and verifying the effectiveness of due diligence. Downstream SMEs should consider establishing permanent business relations with their suppliers as the best means for a continual flow of tracking and verification information.

Step 5: Communicate and report on due diligence

Step 5 provides recommendations on how to externally communicate relevant information on due diligence polices, processes and activities conducted to identify and address actual and potential impacts, including the findings of these actions.

Strategic questions for enterprises to ask

- To what extent are you reporting on policies on child labour and forced labour in your operations and supply chain? Are these reports publicly available?
- What significant adverse impacts or risks have been identified, prioritised and assessed and what are the criteria for prioritisation? Has this been communicated publicly?
- What activities is your company implementing to identify, prevent or mitigate adverse risks and impacts, including timelines and benchmarks for improvement and outcomes? For child labour and forced labour, has an effective system been implemented? Have details of these been shared?
- How is your company measuring and tracking implementation of activities to identify, prevent, cease or mitigate child labour and forced labour? Have the results been shared publicly?
- In instances when you have caused or contributed to an impact, to what extent have you communicated to stakeholders your follow-up actions and results?
- If your company has provided for, or co-operated in, any remediation, what were the results? Has this information been shared publicly?

Communicate and report on due diligence

Companies should communicate externally on their due diligence activities, the risks found – including child labour and forced labour – and the actions that have been taken to address these risks. Such public reporting is increasingly being called for as part of non-financial reporting and in due diligence legislation, as well as voluntary disclosure frameworks by investors. Some jurisdictions may have specific reporting requirements with respect to due diligence.

Publicly report relevant information on due diligence processes

What are you communicating externally?

Clear, accurate and timely information should be provided to affected stakeholders and business partners on actual and potential child labour and forced labour impacts identified, and on the steps and measures you have taken to mitigate or prevent them. Naturally, public company reports should have due regard for commercial confidentiality and other competitive or security concerns.

- **Due diligence policies and management systems:** Relevant information including management structures, staff training and due diligence processes in place, as well as the system of controls and transparency your company has applied or is in the process of applying, throughout the cocoa supply chain (i.e. a chain of custody or traceability system either on its own or in collaboration with other stakeholders).
- **Due diligence process and the supply chain risks:** Reporting should cover the process your company uses to identify, prioritise and assess risks in the cocoa supply chain, and the results of this assessment. In terms of child labour and forced labour this should include measures taken to mitigate and prevent child labour and forced labour in your supply chain. Such external communication may provide the information on measures that will be taken if your company becomes aware of child labour and forced labour in your supply chain, with time bound limits for remedial action and involvement of relevant stakeholders. Public reporting could also include 3rd party assessments on your company's due diligence efforts, any shareable assessments of control

point enterprises in your supply chain, as well as other assessments conducted on segments of your supply chain that are considered at risk for child labour and forced labour.

- **Progress and outcomes:** Reporting could communicate the findings and outcomes of due diligence efforts on what has worked as well as what should be improved.

Box 8. Examples of what to communicate when reporting on progress and outcomes of due diligence efforts

- **The coverage** of a company's due diligence with regards to child labour and forced labour and how this compares to overall sourcing. For example, "our due diligence efforts in 2022 covered 200 households which represents 80% of the direct supply chain and approximately 50% of our total cocoa supply chain (including that from the indirect supply chain)."
- **The number or percentage** of children identified in or at risk of child labour and forced labour through a company's due diligence. For example: In 2022, approximately 27% of children interviewed as part of our due diligence systems were found to be in child labour."
- **The types of support** provided, including information on prevention and remediation support such as awareness raising activities, support to improve access to quality education, income generating activities, etc. For example: "As part of efforts to tackle child labour and forced labour in the cocoa supply chain, 200 households were involved in awareness raising activities, 150 school kits were distributed and 100 households received support for alternative income generating activities."
- **The outcome** of those actions, for example the number of children that are now out of child labour and other changes recorded through follow-up on risks and impacts identified. For example: "A third of children found in child labour are no longer in child labour after two follow-up visits." Or "Child labour has decreased by 30% in the communities we source from."
- **The efficacy and efficiency** of due diligence efforts such as improvements in case identification rates, the speed of support provided, outcomes such as reductions in child labour.

Publish the above information in a way that is easily accessible and appropriate

Reports on a company's due diligence should be easily accessible, for example published on its website, or published through sustainability or integrated reports, available at the enterprise's premises and in local languages. Be aware that communicating with impacted, or potentially impacted, rightsholders may require a different approach than other stakeholders. It is important that communities understand company commitments in terms of actions to address adverse impacts such as child labour and forced labour, what activities will be put in place and why, their outcomes over time, and what recourse an individual may have should those commitments not be met.

Remedy: Provide for or co-operate in remediation when appropriate

The provision of a remedy is a separate, critical process that due diligence should enable and support. This chapter describes different ways a company in the cocoa sector can provide for or co operate in remediation in the case of child labour and forced labour risks and impacts when appropriate.

Provide for or co-operate in remediation when appropriate

Remediation seeks "to restore the affected person or persons to the situation they would be in had the adverse impact not occurred (where possible) and enable remediation that is proportionate to the significance and scale of the adverse impact" (OECD, 2018[3]).

According to the OECD recommendations (Figure 5), when the enterprise identifies that it has **caused** or **contributed to** actual adverse impacts, these impacts should be addressed by the company providing for or co-operating in their remediation.

Remedy may include "apologies, restitution, rehabilitation, financial or non-financial compensation and punitive sanctions (whether criminal or administrative, such as fines), as well as the prevention of harm through, for example, injunctions or guarantees of non-repetition" (OHCHR, 2011[36])

Child labour remediation is about supporting children, their families and communities to remove children from a situation of child labour. In practice many of the activities and support that can be provided to help remove children from a situation of child labour are similar to measures to prevent and mitigate future cases; please see Chapter 3 for more information on prevention and mitigation. Similarly, forced labour remediation is the process of supporting victims (children or adults) to leave situations of forced labour and as far as possible correct the harms experienced by victims. Companies should consult affected persons, including children, adolescents, caregivers, or the family to ensure they understand what is happening and why. Companies should also discuss the type of support required to enable the child to avoid child labour or forced labour.

Examples of remediation for **child labour** include:

a) providing education materials and supporting educational costs (e.g. school kits, uniforms, fees, stipends and other items that can facilitate a child's entry into the education system);

b) contributing towards education support services (e.g. tutoring and bridge classes to children);

c) providing vocational training or apprenticeships.

Where children lack access to quality education, companies could also consider contributing to community interventions such as building critical infrastructure in collaboration with government and local stakeholders. Companies who cause or contribute to the child labour should be ready to provide additional financial or logistical support to support a case referred. Figure 9 provides a decision tree methodology to help companies select support for children and communities.

Examples of remediation for **forced labour** include:

- Restitution to ensure workers are paid back any owed wages or other financial penalties, such as interest on loan payments.
- Compensation for pain and suffering endured.
- Rehabilitation that could include provision such as stipends, legal assistance, assistance with repatriation, if desired.
- Medical care, psychological support or other assistance that the victim, owing to their circumstance, may not be able to access on their own.

Figure 9. How to select support for children and communities

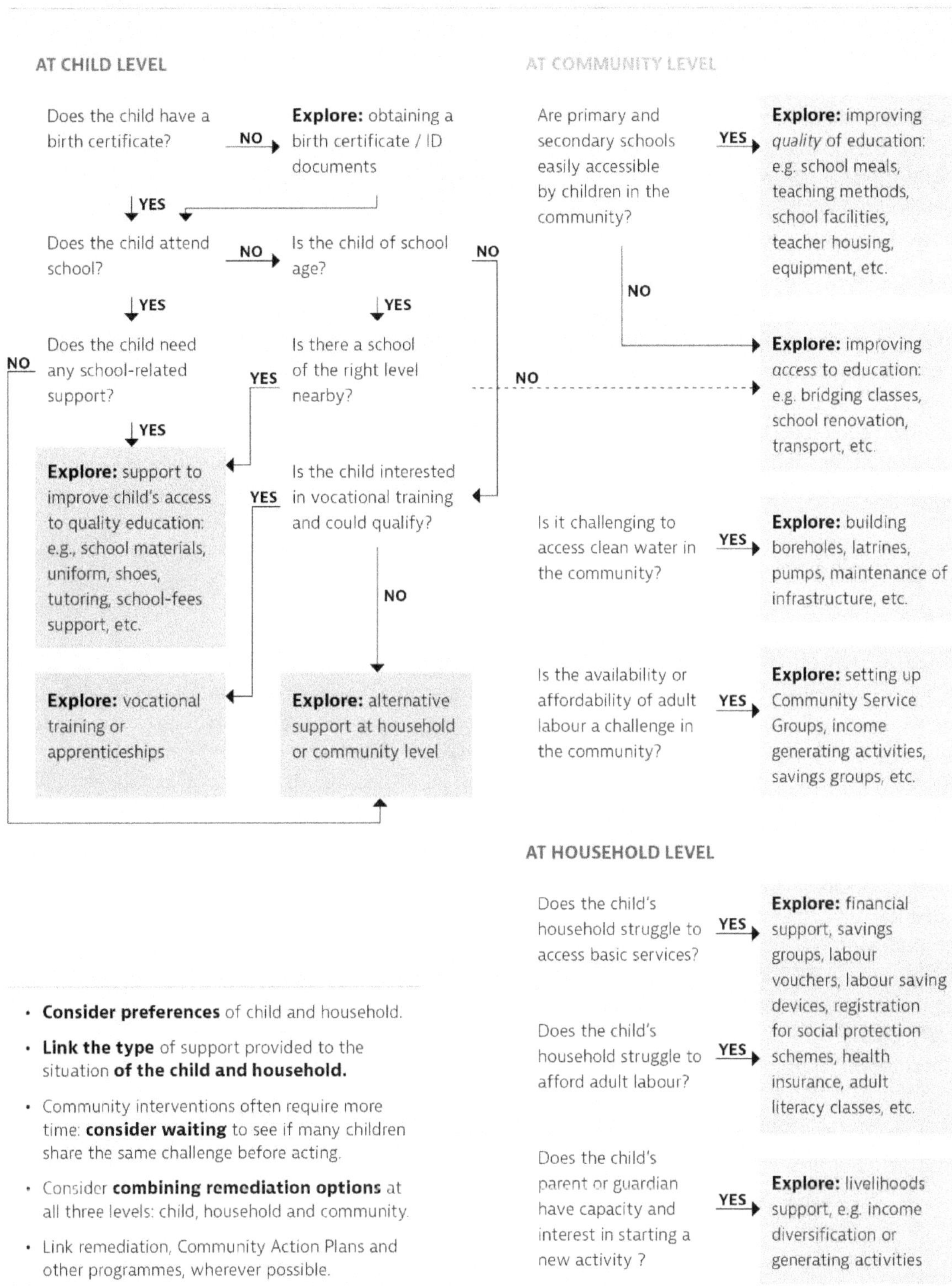

Source: ICI (2022[33]), Decision tree: Selecting support to prevent and remediate child labour through a CLMRS, https://www.cocoainitiative.org/knowledge-hub/resources/selecting-support-prevent-and-remediate-child-labour-through-clmrs

Grievance mechanism

When appropriate, the OECD recommends companies provide for or co-operate with legitimate grievance mechanisms through which impacted stakeholders and rightsholders can raise complaints and seek to have them addressed with the enterprise. These can include both state and non-state processes. In some cases, enterprises may have an obligation to participate in state-based judicial grievance mechanisms or non-judicial mechanisms such as specialist government bodies (see Box 9 on OECD National Contact Points for Responsible Business Conduct as an example), consumer protection agencies, regulatory oversight bodies, or environmental protection agencies. Companies may also co-operate in non-state-based grievance mechanisms, such as a multi-stakeholder grievance mechanism or through Global Framework Agreements between trade unions and multinational companies.

Operational-level grievance mechanisms operated by companies also play an important role in providing access to remedy as they alert companies to suspected adverse impacts that need to be addressed. Examples include in-house worker complaint mechanisms or third-party complaint systems. Operational-level grievance mechanisms should be designed in line with the core effectiveness criteria set out in the UNGPs and the OECD Guidelines which highlight that mechanisms should be legitimate, accessible, predictable, equitable, transparent, rights compatible and a source of continuous learning. In the cocoa sector, companies can work with farming communities to set up grievance focal points. This allows the communities to discuss issues and identify and implement solutions with support from the local farmer groups.

Box 9. Remedy through the OECD National Contact Points for Responsible Business Conduct

The OECD network of National Contact Points for Responsible Business Conduct (NCPs for RBC) are agencies established by governments who have adhered to OECD recommendations on Responsible Business Conduct. Their responsibilities are twofold: to promote the OECD Guidelines and related due diligence guidances, and to contribute to the resolution of issues through a voluntary process called "specific instances". To date, 51 governments have an NCP, and over 620 specific instances have been received by the network.

In 2014, the NGOs, Equitable Cambodia (EC) and Inclusive Development International (IDI), submitted a case ("specific instance") to the NCP of Australia alleging that ANZ Bank had not observed the Guidelines relating to the company's involvement with Phnom Penh Sugar Co. Ltd (PPS) in Cambodia. The Australian NCP considered issues including land seizures, child labour and destruction of crops and property by PPS in relation to a sugar cane plantation for which ANZ Bank had provided financing. Despite undergoing mediation facilitated by the NCP, the parties were unable to reach agreement. Civil society actors on the ground continued to raise the issue of compensation and provided essential support to the NCP to facilitate this during the follow up phase. As a result, the parties re-engaged in discussions and ANZ Bank agreed to provide financial contribution corresponding to the gross profit it earned from this operation to help alleviate the hardships faced by the affected communities and support their efforts toward rehabilitation.

Source: OECD (2020[37]), National Contact Points for Responsible Business Conduct: Providing access to remedy – 20 years and the road ahead, https://mneguidelines.oecd.org/NCPs-for-RBC-providing-access-to-remedy-20-years-and-the-road-ahead.pdf.

Reaching scale and impact to address child labour and forced labour through collaboration

This final chapter explores how companies in the cocoa sector can use collaborative initiatives to support their due diligence efforts and drive systemic change across the sector.

Responsible business conduct and collaborative action in the cocoa sector

Collaboration in implementing due diligence

Industry and multi-stakeholder initiatives can support and strengthen a company's efforts to implement due diligence – whether in developing policies, assessing human rights impacts, or tracking progress at a sectoral level. Such collaboration can pool information on human rights risks and impacts, help increase leverage and scale-up effective measures. It can also increase sector transparency and enable cost-sharing and savings. However, collaboration does not replace the individual company's responsibility to conduct due diligence and identify, prevent and address human rights risks and impacts such as child labour and forced labour.

Collaboration to address systemic challenges for human rights in the cocoa sector

Collaborative approaches are a good way to address root causes and systemic issues and can be supported through:

- **Engagement with governments**: Governments are the key actors to address child labour and forced labour in the cocoa sector. Companies can support government and community efforts by improving supply chain transparency and collaborating on mitigation and remediation efforts. Companies can also engage with regional or national governments to promote laws, policies and measures driving responsible business conduct or the enforcement of laws and regulations.
- **Pooling information and developing shared data systems**: Collaboration with other companies for example can support the development of credible and accessible sources of data on child labour and forced labour in the cocoa sector and its root causes. Making data transparent by participating in public data repositories can strengthen collective knowledge on the issue to effect broader change.
- **Learning from and building on existing initiatives**: Collaborating with other businesses, civil society organisations, governments, international organisations and other stakeholders active in fighting child labour and forced labour can avoid duplication and fragmentation of efforts. Companies can for example consider participating in international efforts to promote child and forced labour free supply chains such as the ILO's Child Labour Platform and Global Business Network on Forced Labour, and ICI. Collaboration can also support co-ordinating different company efforts on CLMRS and help strengthen and improve effectiveness of national systems (UNICEF, 2022[21]).
- **Engaging with children, child rights groups and forced labour experts**: Children and their representatives, as well as representatives of victims of forced labour are a separate and important group to improve a company's own quality of analysis and understanding by filling information gaps and identifying issues that may have been missed by other stakeholders – notably on causes of child labour or forced labour in a given region.
- **Collaborating across sectors**: Collaborating across different sectors (i.e. beyond the cocoa sector) can scale-up effective prevention and mitigation measures and ensure that sector-wide efforts to eliminate child labour and forced labour do not drive children to work in other sectors such other agricultural sectors, artisanal mining, the garment/textile sector or the sex trade.
- **Using a landscape approach**: A landscape approach involve all relevant parties in a given geographic area, such as other companies, civil society organisations, international organisations, national and regional government agencies and multi-stakeholder organisations. They can help address child labour in combination with other related issues such as education, health, water and sanitation and other child protection measures.

Annex A. Glossary of terms

Child labour: The ILO Conventions No. 138 and No. 182 define "child labour" as work that deprives children of their childhood, their potential and their dignity, and that is harmful to their physical or mental development including by interfering with their education by: depriving them of the opportunity to attend school; obliging them to leave school prematurely; or requiring them to attempt to combine school attendance with excessively long and heavy work (ILO, n.d.[6]) (ILO, n.d.[7]). The definition of child labour is both a function of the age of a child, and the nature of work that is being performed (ILO/IOE, 2015[5]).

Forced labour and slavery like practices: According to the ILO Convention No. 29 (ILO, n.d.[10]), forced labour is "all work or service which is exacted from any person under the menace of any penalty and for which the said person has not offered himself voluntarily". Forced labour can apply to both adults and children. Children of adults who are in forced labour are also considered in forced labour. A forced labour situation is determined by the nature of the relationship between a person and an "employer" and not by the type of activity performed (ILO, 2015[38]). Slavery like practices include debt bondage, serfdom and forced marriage.

Forced labour (of children): According to the ILO's operational definition of forced labour of children (ILO, 2012[39]), it is defined as work performed by children under coercion applied by a third party (other than by his or her parents) either to the child or to the child's parents, or work performed by a child as a direct consequence of their parent or parents being engaged in forced labour as defined by the ILO Convention No. 29; or work performed by children in any one of the following worst forms of child labour the ILO Convention No. 182: a) all forms of slavery or practices similar to slavery, such as the sale and trafficking of children, debt bondage, and serfdom, including forced or compulsory recruitment of children for use in armed conflict; b) the use, procuring, or offering of a child for prostitution, for the production of pornography, or for pornographic performances; c) the use, procuring, or offering of a child for illicit activities, in particular for the production and trafficking of drugs as defined in relevant international treaties (ILO/Walk Free/IOM, 2022[15]), (ILO, 2012[39]). The coercion may take place during the child's recruitment, to force the child or his or her parents to accept the job, or once the child is working, to force him/her to do tasks which were not part of what was agreed at the time of recruitment or to prevent the child from leaving the work (ILO, 2012[39]).

Human trafficking, including child trafficking: Trafficking in persons, or human trafficking, can lead to forced labour. It involves the movement of a person, often across international borders, for the purpose of exploitation. A basic definition of human trafficking is found in the "Palermo Protocol" of 2000 (UN, n.d.[40]). Trafficking is constituted of three distinct elements – act, means, and purpose (exploitation). Coercion is one of the means, which states that when coercion (or any other means) is used to get victims into an exploitative situation, actual exploitation need not happen for a trafficking crime to have taken place. For children specifically, child trafficking means the recruitment and or transfer, harbouring, or receipt of children for the purposes of exploitation.

Minimum age: The ILO Convention No. 138 requires countries to establish a minimum age for entry into work or employment, and national policies for the elimination of child labour. It establishes 15 as the minimum age for work in general and 18 as the minimum age for hazardous work, with developing countries given the option of setting a minimum age of 14 as a transitional measure (ILO/IOE, 2015[5]).

Young workers: "Young worker" refers to a person who has reached the minimum legal working age, usually 15, but is under 18 years old (ILO, 2020[41]).

Worst forms of child labour: According to the ILO Convention No. 182 (ILO, n.d.[7]), there are four categories of the worst forms of child labour:

- All forms of slavery or practices similar to slavery, such as the sale, trafficking of children, debt bondage and serfdom or compulsory labour, including forced or compulsory recruitment of children for use in armed conflict
- The use, procuring or offering of a child for prostitution, for the production of pornography or for pornographic performances
- The use, procuring or offering of a child for illicit activities, in particular for the production and trafficking of drugs as defined in the relevant international treaties
- "Hazardous work" which, by its nature or the circumstances in which it is carried out, is likely to harm the health, safety or morals of children. According to this Convention, the precise nature of those tasks that are prohibited are to be defined and reviewed by each country.

References

Alliance 8.7 (2018), *Target 8.7*, https://www.alliance87.org/target-8-7/. [13]

Fairtrade Foundation (2020), *Cocoa Sustainable Livelihoods Landscape Study*, https://www.fairtrade.org.uk/resources-library/researching/commodity-reports/cocoa-sustainable-livelihoods-landscape-study/. [20]

ICCO (2022), "Grindings of Cocoa Beans", *ICCO Quarterly Bulletin of Cocoa Statistics*, https://www.icco.org/statistics/#tab-id-7. [19]

ICCO (2022), *ICCO Quarterly Bulletin of Cocoa Statistics*, https://www.icco.org/statistics/#tab-id-6. [12]

ICCO (n.d.), *Cocoa Economy Information*, https://www.icco.org/economy/ (accessed on 2023). [17]

ICI (2022), *Decision tree: Selecting support to prevent and remediate child labour through a CLMRS*, https://www.cocoainitiative.org/knowledge-hub/resources/selecting-support-prevent-and-remediate-child-labour-through-clmrs. [33]

ICI (2021), *Benchmarking study: Overview and definition of Child Labour Monitoring and Remediation Systems*, https://www.cocoainitiative.org/knowledge-hub/resources/benchmarking-study-overview-and-definition-child-labour-monitoring-and. [25]

ICI (2021), *Risk models for predicting child labour*, https://www.cocoainitiative.org/knowledge-hub/resources/risk-models-predicting-child-labour. [30]

ICI (2020), *Cocoa Barometer 2020*, https://www.cocoainitiative.org/knowledge-hub/resources/2020-cocoa-barometer. [24]

ICI (2019), *Education quality and child labour: A review of evidence from cocoa-growing communities in Côte d'Ivoire and Ghana*, https://www.cocoainitiative.org/knowledge-hub/resources/education-quality-and-child-labour-review-evidence-cocoa-growing. [22]

ICI (2019), *Using community-level data to understand child labour risk in cocoa-growing areas of Côte d'Ivoire and Ghana: Executive Summary*, https://www.cocoainitiative.org/knowledge-hub/resources/using-community-level-data-understand-child-labour-risk-infographic. [27]

ICI (n.d.), *Child Labour Monitoring and Remediation Systems: Introduction*, https://clmrs.cocoainitiative.org/introduction. [26]

ICI (n.d.), *Community Child Labour Risk Assessment - Data Collections Tools*, https://www.cocoainitiative.org/knowledge-hub/resources/community-child-labour-risk-assessment-data-collections-tools. [29]

ICI (n.d.), *Protective Community Index*, https://www.cocoainitiative.org/knowledge-hub/resources/protective-community-index. [28]

ILAB (2022), *List of Goods Produced by Child Labor or Forced Labor*, https://www.dol.gov/agencies/ilab/reports/child-labor/list-of-goods#:~:text=The%20most%20common%20agricultural%20goods,and%20diamonds%20are%20most%20common. [1]

ILO (2020), *Supplier guidance on preventing, identifying and addressing child labour*, https://www.ilo.org/wcmsp5/groups/public/---ed_norm/---ipec/documents/publication/wcms_792211.pdf. [41]

ILO (2018), *Guidelines concerning the measurement of forced labour*, https://www.ilo.org/wcmsp5/groups/public/---dgreports/---stat/documents/meetingdocument/wcms_648619.pdf. [11]

ILO (2015), *Combating forced labour: a handbook for employers and business*, https://www.ilo.org/global/topics/forced-labour/publications/WCMS_101171/lang--en/index.htm. [38]

ILO (2012), *Hard to see, harder to count - Survey guidelines to estimate forced labour of adults and children*, https://www.ilo.org/global/topics/forced-labour/publications/WCMS_182096/lang--en/index.htm. [39]

ILO (n.d.), "C029 - Forced Labour Convention, 1930 (No. 29)", *NORMLEX Information System on International Labour Standards*, https://www.ilo.org/dyn/normlex/en/f?p=NORMLEXPUB:12100:0::NO::P12100_ILO_CODE:C029. [10]

ILO (n.d.), "C138 - Minimum Age Convention, 1973 (No. 138)", *NORMLEX Information System on International Labour Standards*, https://www.ilo.org/dyn/normlex/en/f?p=NORMLEXPUB:12100:::NO:12100:P12100_ILO_CODE:C138:NO. [6]

ILO (n.d.), "C182 - Worst Forms of Child Labour Convention, 1999 (No. 182)", *NORMLEX Information System on International Labour Standards*, https://www.ilo.org/dyn/normlex/en/f?p=NORMLEXPUB:12100:::NO:12100:P12100_ILO_CODE:C182:NO. [7]

ILO/IOE (2015), *How to do business with respect for children's right to be free from child labour: ILO-IOE child labour guidance tool for business*, https://www.ilo.org/ipec/Informationresources/WCMS_IPEC_PUB_27555/lang--en/index.htm. [5]

ILO/UNICEF (2021), *Child Labour: Global estimates 2020, trends and the road forward*, https://www.ilo.org/ipec/Informationresources/WCMS_797515/lang--en/index.htm. [14]

ILO/Walk Free/IOM (2022), *Global Estimates Of Modern Slavery: Forced Labour And Forced Marriage*, https://www.walkfree.org/reports/global-estimates-of-modern-slavery-2022/. [15]

Kozicka M., Tacconi F. , Horna D. , Gotor E. (2018), *Forecasting Cocoa Yields for 2050*, Bioversity International, https://hdl.handle.net/10568/93236. [18]

Myers, A. (2019), *New space satellite tech set to help cocoa traceability in West Africa*, https://www.confectionerynews.com/Article/2019/04/12/New-space-satellite-tech-set-to-help- [35]

cocoa-traceability-in-West-Africa.

OECD (2020), *National Contact Points for Responsible Business Conduct: Providing access to remedy - 20 years and the road ahead*, https://mneguidelines.oecd.org/NCPs-for-RBC-providing-access-to-remedy-20-years-and-the-road-ahead.pdf. [37]

OECD (2018), *OECD Due Diligence Guidance for Responsible Business Conduct*, http://mneguidelines.oecd.org/OECD-Due-Diligence-Guidance-for-Responsible-Business-Conduct.pdf. [3]

OECD (2011), *OECD Guidelines for Multinational Enterprises*, https://doi.org/10.1787/9789264115415-en. [32]

OECD/EU/ILO (2019), *Responsible Business: Key Messages from International Instruments*, https://mneguidelines.oecd.org/Brochure-responsible-business-key-messages-from-international-instruments.pdf. [42]

OECD/FAO (2021), *OECD-FAO Guidance for Responsible Agricultural Supply Chain: Helping achieve the Sustainable Development Goals*, https://www.fao.org/documents/card/en/c/CA7970EN/. [4]

OECD/FAO (2016), *OECD-FAO Guidance for Responsible Agricultural Supply Chains*, OECD Publishing, Paris, https://doi.org/10.1787/9789264251052-en. [2]

OHCHR (2011), *Guiding Principles on Business and Human Rights*, https://www.ohchr.org/en/publications/reference-publications/guiding-principles-business-and-human-rights. [36]

Sadhu, S. (2020), *Assessing Progress in Reducing Child Labor in Cocoa Growing Areas of Côte d'Ivoire and Ghana*, https://www.norc.org/PDFs/Cocoa%20Report/NORC%202020%20Cocoa%20Report_English.pdf. [9]

Shift, IOE (2019), *SMEs and the Responsibility to Respect Human Rights*, https://shiftproject.org/resource/smes-and-the-responsibility-to-respect-human-rights/. [34]

SÜDWIND e.V. (2021), *Guide to conducting risk analyses for cocoa producing countries*, https://www.kakaoforum.de/en/news-service/news/news-detail/guide-to-conducting-risk-analyses-for-cocoa-producing-countries-published-843/. [31]

Tulane University, Walk Free Foundation (2018), *The prevalence of forced labour and child labour in the cocoa sectors of Côte d'Ivoire and Ghana*, https://www.cocoainitiative.org/knowledge-hub/resources/walk-free-foundation-study-prevalence-forced-labour-and-child-labour-cocoa. [16]

UN (n.d.), "Convention on the Rights of the Child", *United Nations Treaty Collection*, https://treaties.un.org/pages/ViewDetails.aspx?src=IND&mtdsg_no=IV-11&chapter=4&clang=_en. [8]

UN (n.d.), "Protocol to Prevent, Suppress and Punish Trafficking in Persons, Especially Women and Children, supplementing the United Nations Convention against Transnational Organized Crime", *United Nations Treaty Collection*, https://treaties.un.org/Pages/ViewDetails.aspx?src=ind&mtdsg_no=XVIII-12-a&chapter=18&clang=_en. [40]

UNICEF (2022), *Child labour and responsible business conduct: A guidance note for action*, https://www.unicef.org/reports/child-labour-and-responsible-business-conduct. [21]

UNICEF (2018), *Children's Rights in the Cocoa-Growing Communities of Côte d'Ivoire: Synthesis Report*, https://sites.unicef.org/csr/css/synthesis-report-children-rights-cocoa-communities-en.pdf. [23]

Notes

[1] To learn more, read Inter-Sectoral Standard Operating Procedures for Child Protection and Family Welfare: Guidelines, Tools and Forms for Casework and Management published by the Ministry of Gender, Children and Social Protection of Ghana in 2020 at https://www.unicef.org/ghana/media/3286/file/Inter-Sectoral%20SOPs%20for%20Child%20Protection%20and%20Family%20Welfare.pdf

[2] The three main reference points for responsible business are the ILO Tripartite Declaration of Principles concerning Multinational Enterprises and Social Policy, the OECD Guidelines for Multinational Enterprises and the UN Guiding Principles on Business and Human Rights. These international instruments are aligned with, and complementary to, each other (OECD/EU/ILO, 2019[42]).

[3] To find additional resources on the ICI's website, visit https://www.cocoainitiative.org/knowledge-hub/resources/additional-resources-support-human-rights-due-diligence-cocoa-sector

[4] For further information, visit https://www.dol.gov/agencies/ilab/resources/reports/child-labor

[5] For further information on gender responsive due diligence, visit https://www.genderduediligence.org/

[6] OECD recommendations underscore that obeying domestic laws in the jurisdictions in which the enterprise operates and/or where they are domiciled is the first obligation of enterprises.

[7] See OECD-FAO Guidance (OECD/FAO, 2016[2]) p.20 Figure 1.1. on the various stages of agricultural supply chains and enterprises involved.

[8] For further details, see Box 5. Engagement with business relationships operating at control points in the supply chain of the OECD Due Diligence Guidance (OECD, 2018[3]) and page 38 of the OECD-FAO Guidance (OECD/FAO, 2016[2]).

[9] To learn more about OECD Alignment Assessment, visit https://www.oecd.org/corporate/industry-initiatives-alignment-assessment.htm

www.ingramcontent.com/pod-product-compliance
Lightning Source LLC
Chambersburg PA
CBHW061225240926
51846CB00006B/1355